shibori knits

shibori knits

The Art of Exquisite Felted Knits

Gina Wilde

Foreword by Yoshiko Iwamoto Wada

POTTER
CRAFT
New York

for Austin, always.

Published in the United States by Potter Craft,
an imprint of the Crown Publishing Group,
a division of Random House, Inc., New York.
www.crownpublishing.com
www.pottercraft.com

POTTER CRAFT and CLARKSON N. POTTER are trademarks,
and POTTER and colophon are registered trademarks of
Random House, Inc.

Thanks to the Craft Yarn Council of America
(www.yarnstandards.com) for their Standard Yarn Weight System
Chart, which appears on page 124

Library of Congress Cataloging-in-Publication Data
is available upon request

ISBN 978-0-307-39354-8

Printed in China

Design by Chi Ling Moy

1 3 5 7 9 10 8 6 4 2

First Edition

contents

foreword
6

preface
8

introduction
10

chapter one *surrender to shibori*
elegant explorations in knitting and felting possibility
16

chapter two *shibori creativity*
experiments in unlikely combinations of fiber
42

chapter three *subtle shibori*
adventures in color, composition, and construction
80

appendix
118

Technical Shibori Felting Concepts
118

Tips and Advice for Successful Shibori
120

Glossary
121

yarn substitution guide
122

Alchemy retailers
123

index
128

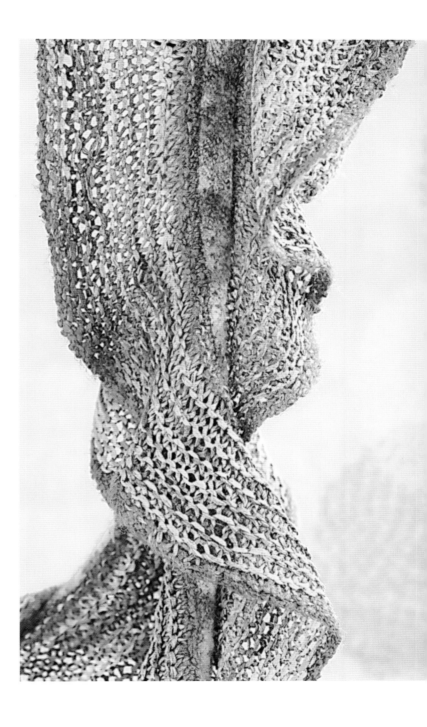

foreword

Shibori has grown far beyond its traditional roots in Japan. Since I introduced the art form to artists in the West in 1975, shibori has grown to encompass something much larger than its original concept of shaped-resist dyeing, particularly in its widening interpretations of shape manipulation and cloth transformation. It's easy to see why. At its essence, shibori stems from a dimensional transformation—from a 2-D plane to 3-D resist shape, which is then exposed to dye. The resulting dye pattern is a permanent memory of the manipulative processes applied to the fabric. The expansion of this definition is a testament to the artist's adventurous imagination and understanding of shibori's magical process.

The creative impulse for dimensional change is fertile ground for a variety of fields—art, textiles, and fashion—and can be interpreted in a number of different media, such as dyeing, weaving, and now knitting. Almost any knitter can identify with the unexpected horror of discovering an adult-sized sweater suddenly shrunken, child-sized. Such is the outcome of wool knitwear that takes an accidental spin in the wash. But controlled transformation opens one up to new dimensions and startlingly beautiful designs without veering from the basic precepts of knitting. Shibori is an empowering tool for knitters; it's a method for introducing possibility and also asks that a bit of risk be taken—like an adventure where the destination is new personal expression.

Wool is a beautiful yarn for knitting, as is silk. While both are protein fibers, each behaves quite differently when exposed to water and agitation. Gina's sophisticated understanding of each yarn's behavior and the shibori process allows her great creative flexibility in her knit designs. She capitalizes on wool's magic by setting it against other natural fibers of very different properties and then deftly applying shibori to highlight the qualitative differences between them. One is allowed to shine against the other. The result is a beautiful, dimensional transformation of material. Knitting her own pieces, Gina makes her own art canvases at will. With her great eye for color and quality of hand, she selects yarns to make a texturally interesting, colorful painting one can wear or live with.

Now with this book, knitters are invited to apply their craft in a new way by venturing into the world of shibori. Gina offers a broad basis for this exploration and gives guidance for transformative knitting. She provides systematic instruction, vivid and rich use of color, and clear explanations of choices that will appeal to all levels of ability. Most important, *Shibori Knits* is sure to inspire adventurous creativity in any knitter.

—Yoshiko Iwamoto Wada,
President of the World Shibori Network—World

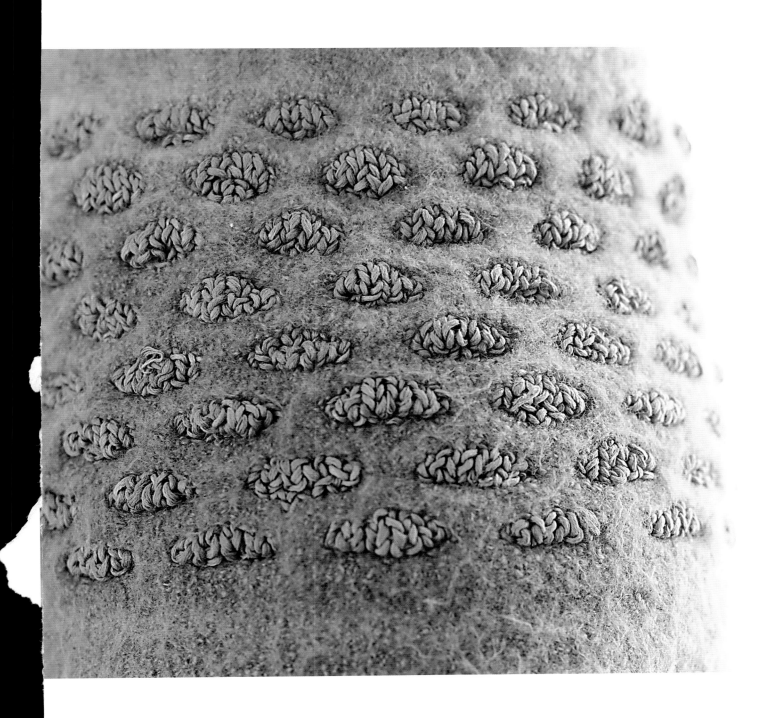

preface

A Chance Meeting

What happens when you take a luxury fiber that's not supposed to felt, knit something lovely, then throw it in the washing machine and felt it anyway? What could be an unfortunate knitting accident instead becomes a wonderful opening into a new and dynamic fiber expression. Such was my introduction to shibori.

When my daughter received an opportunity to study puppet making in the Czech Republic, I whipped up a fast pair of hand warmers. She would be spending many hours daily carving wood in a snow-covered barn outside Prague, and from my perspective, warm but nimble hands seemed a prerequisite for this creative task. From stash yarns, I pulled a DK weight silk/merino blend, and for fun, added a cuff embellishment using two different silk yarns—one boucle, the other a smooth single ply. Weeks after her return from Eastern Europe, when my daughter finally emptied her backpack, one of the hand warmers inadvertently made its way into the washable pile of clothes. Pulling one wet hand warmer out of the washer, I braced myself for knit disaster—until I saw what had happened. The silk/merino blend felted beautifully, and now had an exquisite halo with an ethereal texture and sheen. The cuff, made from two kinds of silk fiber, didn't felt—it ruffled. Delighted, I called out to my daughter, "Where's your other hand warmer? Let's felt it!"

Felted shibori knitting is a spectacular collision of chance and happy accident, where the precision of knitting meets the magic of shaped-resist felting.

The happy accident that created these hand warmers (page 88), above, opened the door to my personal shibori exploration. Spirals and ruffles are two of the wonderful textures possible with shibori, as seen in the Portrait Scarf (page 110), at right.

introduction

Something old is new again. Often, the revival of a past tradition brings forth opportunity for fresh perspective. We see this spirit of revival time and again in art, music, fashion, history, politics, philosophy, and more. The concept of shibori has been around for centuries; however, the adaptation of shibori to knitting is new. Building upon the very popular practice of felting, shibori now expands the opportunities to create unique and sophisticated knitwear.

Shibori is a word that drifts through the knitting consciousness with a wide range of interpretation, myriad perceptions, and, possibly, a sprinkle of misunderstanding. Essentially, shibori is a means of embellishing fabric—whether by binding, shaping, twisting, dyeing, or otherwise manipulating textile in order to facilitate change. Qualities of drape, movement, and translucency are associated with shibori knitting, changing the way we look at felted knitting.

There is always a quality of surprise when working with shibori—an understanding that some element of control is surrendered. Still, there are easy-to-use techniques that corral the effects of chance and successful ways to encourage certain behavioral characteristics of fiber in order to obtain fascinating and beautiful results.

A Brief History

An ancient Japanese art dating to at least the eighth century, *shibori* has been used primarily in association with weaving and often incorporates sophisticated dyeing methods. Variations on shibori abound in South America, Africa, India, and Southeast Asia with each region affecting the overall tradition in unique ways. A popular interpretation of shibori surfaced in the 1960s, when many individuals embraced the hand-wrought

clothing expressions of *tie and dye*. Such colorful clothing became widely adopted as the textile calling card of hippies worldwide—the celebrated *tie-dye* revolution. However, there is much more to shibori, and textile artists around the world continue to explore the fascinating tradition.

Types of Shibori Knitting

There are many ways to incorporate shibori into your knitting. This book will focus on three primary methods, each of which works with fiber in a particular way to create many different and beautiful results.

Shape-Resist Felting

The simplest method of shibori calls for combining a felting fiber with a hard object or *resist* (like a handful of marbles or golf balls). Using small rubber bands, the knit fabric is secured around the hard shapes and then washed with the resists in place. After the knit material dries, the resists are removed. The fabric felts in the areas that surround the resists, but not where the hard shapes were once tied. What is left is not only an inter-

Sand records action (tide and wind) over time, just as shibori is a record of alteration over time.

The passage of time and interaction between different forms is visible in nature and can be applied to shibori.

esting piece of shape-resist felting fabric, rendered bumpy with texture, it's also a recording of time—a memory of when the resists were inside the fabric.

Nonfelting Fibers as Resists

Different fibers respond in different ways to felting—some yarns change dramatically and others do not. If you knit together a fiber that will felt (a wool or mohair fiber) with a fiber that does not fuse and shrink (silk, cotton, or bamboo), the two yarn types, when put through the felting process, play off one another to create a new fabric with great texture and depth. By playing with stitch patterns in the two kinds of fiber, such as slip stitches and intarsia, you can create windowpane effects, lace, and even strips of fabric that look like weaving.

Changing Knit Direction

In shibori weaving, the warp and the weft, which run perpendicular to one another, are often worked in a combination of felting and nonfelting fibers to create lush dimensional pieces.

This attractive technique is achieved in knitting by working a narrow strip in felting fiber, and then picking up stitches along the sides with a nonfelting fiber. Spirals, ruffles, flowing edges, and wavy lines are a few contours to expect when you change knit direction. Add beads for embellishment if you please, or incorporate the shape-resist method and the nonfelting fiber technique, and you've expanded the possibility for even more sophisticated shibori knits.

Shibori and Nature

The *action* of shibori is clearly illustrated in nature. Imagine a sandy beach. The sand is rippled in accordance with the rhythm of the tide and the wind. There may be indentations on the surface where birds have walked, a dog has run, or a person has strolled. The consequence of time and action is recorded in the sand. Even a simple shell in the sand acts as a tiny resist, changing the way the mighty ocean finds its way to and from the shore.

Think about the way strata can be seen in rock, how layers of time are encased in each visible line. Moss grows on the rock, winding along the surface of the hard stone, adapting its shape to blend with that upon which it rests. Time is encapsulated, and transformation is visible in both stone and moss. Where I live in Sonoma County, California, the wind blows hard from the west, directly from the nearby Pacific Ocean. Most of the trees look as though they are perpetually reaching to the east, even on days when the wind is still. Again, the passage of time is recorded in nature, and the effects of the alchemical elements—fire, water, earth, and air—are the methods of transformation. The same action is visible in felted shibori knitting.

Shibori and Transformation

It takes courage to knit something and felt it—not knowing exactly what will happen. This is a good metaphor, one of those knitting analogies that makes perfect sense when applied to the non-knitting areas of our lives. We have to let go of knowing sometimes. It is hard to do, but it's the place where something unexpected and magical can happen—where we might fall more deeply in love with what we get rather than what we simply expected.

To work with felted shibori knitting, it is important to understand yarns and their unique qualities. Generally speaking, most fibers behave in predictable ways. Some yarns shrink when felted (also known as fulling); others do not. By harnessing these natural tendencies, very interesting things happen, especially when we combine fibers that behave in different ways. A simple working knowledge of what fibers tend to do when felted is a key to shibori success—the way to unlock many of the mysteries held within this fascinating technique.

Basic resist felting—marbles in a wool square—is a simple method of knit shibori. However, shibori transformation also occurs when protein fibers that felt (such as merino, alpaca, cashmere, mohair, and angora) are worked together with silk proteins, cellulose or plant fibers (such as cotton, linen, and bamboo), or synthetic fibers (such as nylon and polyester) that do not felt. Because wool/animal proteins felt and the silk proteins and cellulose fibers do not, the qualities of each fiber play with and against one other to create remarkable textures. Ruffles, bumps, flowing edges, waving lines, and spirals are a few of the contours one can expect when combining felting and nonfelting fibers together in shibori.

When we think about felting, it's hard not to be restricted by conventions of technique as contemporary fiber artists and knitters generally understand them. For instance, it's not customary to use a wool/silk blend as a felting fiber. Felt silk? Preposterous! Most folks feel more comfortable felting with wool and/or mohair. Another widely held rule about felting is that success is achieved when a fiber is double stranded—the idea is that the two strands of fiber will fuse with one another to form a stronger fabric. What may not be as well known is that a single strand of fiber will felt with remarkably different results. Though still wonderfully strong, there exists the possibility to create fabric that is detailed and lightweight, with incredible nuance.

Natural luxury fibers and handpainted yarns are normally not associated with felting. Yet such fibers offer unique and elegant qualities to the shibori experience. As the creative director of Alchemy Yarns, the fibers depicted in the book are yarns that I have painted myself (which is yet another manifestation of shibori), and, therefore, are the yarns I know intimately. By letting go of some standard assumptions about fiber and embracing a new twist on an old tradition, the shibori practice offers a helpful map to create a radically new finished fabric, something

The Poet's Shawl (page 76) showcases the harmony of shibori, artfuly balancing felting and nonfelting fibers.

lighter, more subtle and ethereal than what is typically associated with felted knitting.

Lifetimes may be spent in exploration of shibori, with generations of knowledge sacredly passed down in families and across cultures. With all respect to such artistry, I offer the results of my knitting adventure—this curious intersection of shibori and knitting—and hope to inspire you to discover the exquisite art of felted shibori knitting.

Understanding Fiber for Shibori Knitting

The patterns in this book will generally list two types of fiber: *felting* and *nonfelting*. If you choose to substitute fibers other than what is recommended, there are important factors to keep in mind. Please find adequate substitutes for both types of fibers, felting and nonfelting. Some patterns will detail only one fiber, usually a felting fiber. To substitute successfully and to achieve the best results, please pay close attention to two factors: *yarn weight* and *yarn content*.

Yarn weight

Be sure to follow the recommended *yarn weight* for each piece, which is detailed under *materials* for each pattern. If the pattern calls for a specific weight fiber, please make every effort to substitute that weight fiber. Should you choose to use a different weight, you will have to make the gauge calculations necessary for that substitution.

Yarn content

There are different factors for felting and nonfelting fibers to consider if you choose to make yarn content substitutions.

Felting Fiber Substitutions

The felting fibers used in this book are almost exclusively blended fibers. One of the qualities that makes shibori unique is that shibori does not rely on typical felting fibers of all wool or wool/mohair blends. Instead, the designs included here and in most disciplines of traditional shibori embrace the qualities only silk can deliver. So you will find that most of the felting fibers suggested are wool/silk blends or mohair/silk blends. If you choose to substitute felting fibers, please pay close attention to a few important properties.

For best results, if the instruction calls for a fiber that is a blend of 60% mohair and 40% silk, make every effort to work with a fiber that is close to that percentage of mohair to silk. For instance, a fiber that is 70% mohair and 30% silk would be a fine substitute. A fiber that is 70% silk and 30% mohair would *not* be a working alternative.

The key thing to remember about felting fibers is that there must be a larger *percentage* of felting fibers (wool/animal protein) than nonfelting fibers (silk protein, cotton, bamboo, or synthetic fiber). Don't use a 50% silk, 50% wool yarn and hope for a good outcome. However, you could use a 60% wool, 40% silk blend and expect things to turn out well.

So read those yarn labels carefully! For felting fibers, choose fiber blends that are made predominantly of wool/animal proteins—merino, mohair, alpaca, angora, and other *all-natural fibers* that are animal protein (excluding silk proteins). Again, pay attention

to percentage in the blends. A great reference on understanding fibers is *The Knitter's Book of Yarn*, by Clara Parkes.

Nonfelting Fiber Substitutions

Let's say a pattern calls for a 100% silk bouclé for the nonfelting fiber. You go to your local yarn store or find something fabulous online, but it's not silk bouclé. Instead, you fall in love with a silk chenille, a 100% bamboo, or even a crunchy, cool cotton. As long as the yarn weight is equivalent to the yarn in the pattern, you can go with your preference. The key is that you don't substitute a wool, wool blend, or any *felting* fiber for the nonfelting fiber. What makes so many of the shibori designs work is that some of the fibers felt and some of them don't. The place where those fibers meet makes a successful shibori piece. Feel free to substitute whatever makes you happy, as long as it is not a felting fiber, and, again, make sure the yarn weight matches!

It is *imperative* that you distinguish between the two categories of fibers: felting and nonfelting. Once you have absorbed that information and as long as you keep the yarn weights consistent with the pattern recommendation, you should be golden with your substitutions. For more information about understanding shibori fiber and making substitutions, please read the Appendix (page 118).

A last word about yarn substitutions

Be aware that, by making substitutions, you might produce a finished piece that is quite different from what is pictured. For instance, if you choose to make the Wine Lover's Scarf (page 32) out of pure wool, you may not get the sheen that is a natural characteristic of the recommended silk/mohair fiber. Though you can successfully substitute one protein fiber for another (wool for silk/mohair), the finished piece will not be exactly the same.

Swatching Information

You read this in every knitting book: Make a swatch!

Swatches are maps—little microcosms of what will happen in the big knit picture. It is always important to make a swatch, even if you use the exact fiber called for in the instructions. We all have different hands and knit with various tensions.

Follow the swatching standard to determine gauge: If your swatch measures smaller that what's given in the gauge recommendation, move up a needle size. If your swatch is larger, move down a needle size. Remember that, as a general rule, a fairly loose hand is usually best for felted knitting. Having a little more space around each stitch allows for a more fused finished fabric. Don't hesitate to adjust needle size to obtain gauge.

More importantly, because most of the pieces in this book call for felting the finished knit, it is imperative to felt the swatch, following the detailed instructions in the Appendix (page 118). All swatch information listed in the materials is given in prefelting measurements. The swatch is meant to help you recognize the characteristics of your fiber, especially if you are felting. Pay attention to (and make notes on) how long you felt the swatch, the number of sessions in the washing machine needed to successfully transform the swatch, and how it changes after drying. This information will be helpful to you when you make the full garment. Post-felting measurements for swatches are not given, because so many factors will determine how your work felts, including the hardness of your water, water temperature, the detergent used, and, of course, the fibers in play.

Exploring shibori is an adventurous journey.

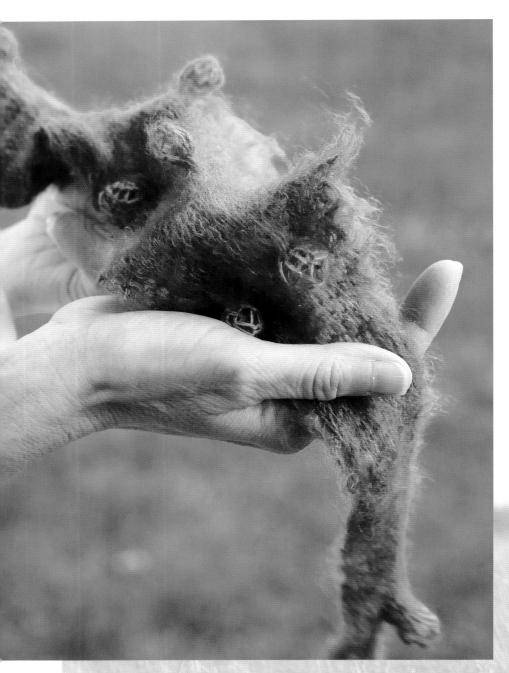

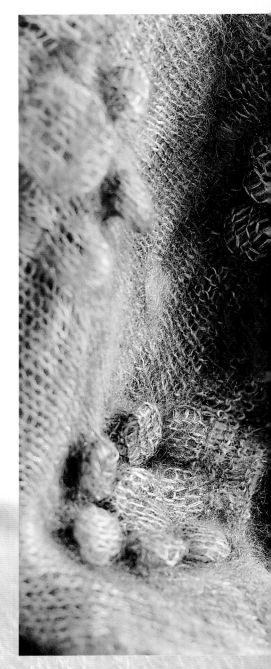

Memory is created in these simple resist felting projects—the Happy Colored Marbles Scarf (page 24), the Bouquet Wrap (page 20), and the Wine Lover's Scarf (page 32).

surrender to *shibori*

Bouquet Wrap **20**

Happy Colored Marbles Scarf **24**

Wood Grain Scarf **28**

Wine Lover's Scarf **32**

Koi Bag **36**

elegant explorations in knitting and
felting possibility

surrender to *shibori*   elegant explorations in shibori possibility

This chapter is about letting go. From a technical knitting perspective, it's about dropping preconceived notions of what constitutes felting fiber and discovering which fibers are good for the shibori purpose. It's about understanding a new kind of felted fiber—an ethereal, light fabric that is created using a blend of ancient and contemporary techniques. The chapter is also a synthesis of simple shapes, sound advice on understanding resist shibori, and harnessing the natural tendencies of fiber to create absolutely original knit designs. The pieces are fun, functional, and, generally speaking, use minimal fiber.

From a metaphorical perspective, this chapter is about surrendering to not knowing. The human animal seems to have a need for control, order, and organization—some of us more than others. There is an understandable desire for knowing the place of things and the outcome of situations. We like to measure space and time, and we like to know what is going to happen—at least we do for many events and circumstances in our lives. Yet, despite our longings, we don't know everything. There are surprises, changes, unforeseen events, disasters—really, life is one surprise after another.

Simultaneously, there are the happy chances and beautiful accidents that keep life full of wonder. Not knowing the outcome is what makes going to the movies or reading a novel so exciting. Chance creates the unmitigated thrill of being in a museum in a foreign city on exactly the same day and at precisely the same time as someone you haven't seen in twenty years. It's the mystery of why my oldest daughter was born exactly on her due date—my parents' wedding anniversary. Or why my youngest child was born in a swirl of family fluctuation and ritual that included a wedding, a death, a funeral, and a birth within the span of five days. Chance or divine inspiration—I don't know.

The beauty of not knowing allows us to experience what is new, exciting, and unexpected. Obviously, with risk comes reward; adventure comes in such a cloak, as well. This chapter is about going on an adventure. The shibori adventure is like a well-planned and exciting boat tour down a beautiful river in South America with a very skilled guide: There are ample provisions on board for a small group of friendly passengers, the departure and arrival times are neatly met, and yet there is unexpected beauty around every twist and turn in the river. Shibori is not meant to be the knitting equivalent of being lost in the wild alone, with dusk approaching and strange sounds rustling in the grasses nearby. It's an adventure, yes—but a controlled adventure. There are safe perimeters within which you can explore shibori in all its glory, but you won't fall off the boat. On my studio wall, I wrote in big letters: *Conceive, believe, achieve.* By following a few simple guidelines, you, too, can conceive beautiful shibori knitting, believe in your ability to make such work, and achieve success.

Memory is created in fabric by utilizing ancient shibori techniques in simple resist felting projects. You will learn to let go when you drop the knit in the washing machine for the first time, shut the door, and let the agitation do its work. A short time later, you will surrender to the moment by opening the door and retrieving the work—transformed into something completely new. You will have controlled many of the factors, so you will have some idea of what to expect, but hopefully the new piece will take on a quality that is even more ethereal, impressive, and beautiful than you could have imagined.

So let go. Surrender to not knowing. Let yourself be amazed by all the beauty and unexpected delight found in embracing a new perspective. Welcome to the shibori adventure. May it infuse your life with all sorts of applicable and meaningful metaphor.

This version of the Happy Colored Marbles Scarf (page 24) uses golf balls as the resist.

bouquet wrap

Something about knitters and flowers just go together. I suppose there are similarities in the way we approach the two creative tasks— the process of planting and tending a garden is quite like plotting and making a knit garment. Similarly, once the garden is planted, it's a treat to share the beauty of flowers, vegetables, trees, and more growing things with friends and family, much in the way a finished knit piece is shared. Knitting and flowers—the fruits of our "labor," the wonderful things we can make with our hands.

Flat glass pieces, or cabochons, commonly used as vase fillers in flower arrangements, are used to create the resist in this elegant wrap. Given the irregular shapes of the cabochons, the finished fabric is a fantastic three-dimensional form, generously sized, and wonderfully original. Make more or fewer flower shapes to suit your desires.

Level Easy

Knitted Measurements

Before felting

Width 24" (61 cm)

Length 72" (183 cm)

After felting

Width 18" (46 cm)

Length 54" (137 cm)

Materials

Felting fiber

6 skeins of Alchemy Yarns Haiku, 60% mohair, 40% silk, ⅞ oz (25g), 325 yds (297m), 43 c Waterlily, **2** fine

Knitting needle in size US 9 (4mm) or size needed to obtain gauge

Approximately 185 rubber bands

Approximately 160 small glass cabochons, each approximately 1" (2.5cm) in diameter

Approximately 23 large glass cabochons, each approximately 1½" (4 cm) in diameter

Tapestry needle

Gauge

16 stitches and 20 rows = 4" (10cm) in stockinette stitch before felting

Notes

Cabochons are available in the floral section of your local craft store in various sizes.

Yarn is worked double throughout. Please refer to the sidebar on page 27 for detailed instructions on easy winding of a double-stranded skein.

Read the section on resists carefully for helpful tips.

I recommend dry cleaning the finished piece to keep the resist shapes intact.

WRAP

Using 2 strands held together, cast on 100 stitches. Knit 8 rows to form border.

Next 2 rows

Row 1 (Right Side) Knit.

Row 2 K4, p92, k4.

Repeat these 2 rows until the piece measures 71" (182 cm), ending after a wrong-side row. Knit 8 rows. Bind off all stitches.

FINISHING

Use a tapestry needle to weave in all the loose ends, being sure to weave at least 3" (7.5cm) of each end to ensure a tight hold during the felting process.

Resist

Lay the wrap on a flat surface, preferably where the entire piece can lie level (I use the floor). To determine position of flowers, place a large cabochon about 10" (25cm) in from the bottom left corner on *top* of the work. Lay 6 to 8 smaller cabochons in a circle around the large piece, leaving approximately 1" (2.5cm) between each cabochon.

Once you are satisfied with the placement, move the resist to the wrong side of the work (under the knit fabric), and secure a rubber band tightly around the resist from the right side of the work. Repeat for additional flowers. Remember that setting in the resist takes up precious yardage of your knit garment, as the knit gathers around the resist, so place the flowers approximately 5–6" (12–15cm) apart to ensure you will have a generously sized garment after felting.

Felting

Please refer to the guidelines for *washing machine felting* on page 118.

Because of the glass cabochons, this piece is quite heavy with all the resists in place. Be prepared for a lot of noise from your washing machine.

I suggest laying out a large towel by your machine. When the piece is ready to come out, move it quickly and carefully to the towel. The towel will not only catch the excess water, it will help you support the piece from underneath to avoid excessive stretching.

Once the felting cycle is done, allow the piece to dry with all the resists inside the fabric. Remove the resists after the piece is totally dry. Remove resists, preferably with your hands, using a scissor only if necessary (being careful not to cut the fabric).

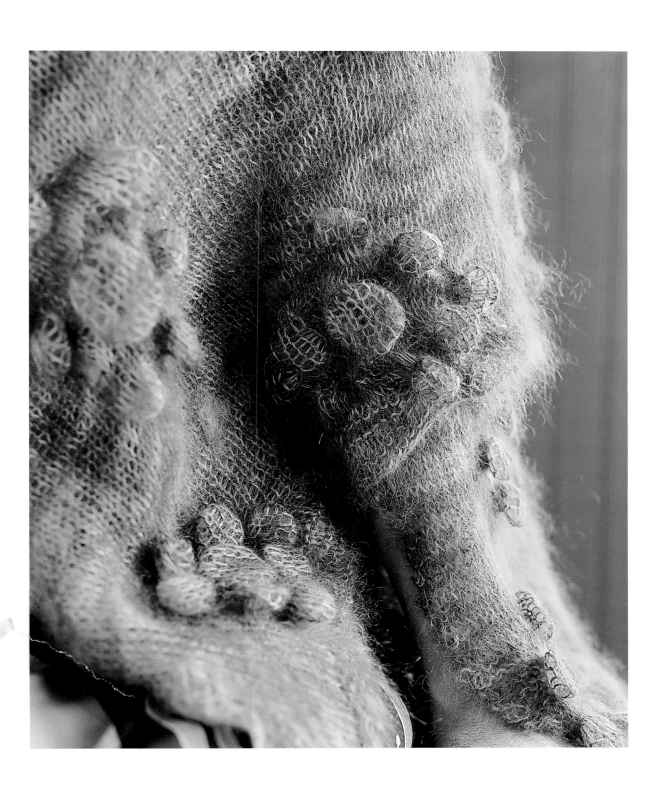

The marble felting technique has successfully

infiltrated the knitting world. For years,

various interpretations

of this ancient and most basic shibori

technique have floated around

on the Internet,

appeared at the odd sheep and wool festival,

and even debuted on Broadway in the wildly

imaginative costumes of

The Lion King.

The simple resist of marbles is used in one

scarf (red/burgundy) and rubber golf balls

are used in another (green/blue). Experiment

with dried beans, eucalyptus pods, buttons,

or any other hard object that can

endure the washing machine

and a whole lotta

shakin' going on!

Level Easy

Knitted Measurements

Before felting

82" x 7" (208cm x 18cm)

After felting

69" x 4" (175cm x 10cm)

Materials

Felting fiber

1 skein each of Alchemy Yarns Haiku, 60% mohair, 40% silk, ⅞ oz (25g), 325 yds (297m). The scarf on page 27 uses 15c Grass Harp (color A) and 03c Lovely Good (color B). The scarf on page 24 uses 25c Aubergine (color A) and 33c Red Run (color B). ❷ fine

Knitting needles in size US 9 (5.5mm) or size needed to obtain gauge

Approximately 30 rubber bands

Approximately 30 marbles or 15 rubber golf balls

Tapestry needle

Gauge

16 stitches and 20 rows = 4" (10cm) in stockinette stitch with yarn held double, before felting

Notes

Gauge is not critical for this garment.

Yarn is held double throughout. Please refer to the sidebar on the opposite page for detailed instructions on easy winding of a double-stranded skein.

I recommend dry cleaning the finished piece to keep the resist shape intact.

SCARF

Using 2 strands of color A held together, cast on 3 stitches.

Row 1 (Right Side) K1, kfb, knit to the end—4 stitches.

Row 2 Knit.

Repeat these 2 rows twice more—6 stitches.

Next 2 rows

Row 1 K1, kfb, knit to the end—7 stitches.

Row 2 K3, purl to the last 3 stitches, k3.

Repeat these 2 rows 23 more times—30 stitches.

Next 2 rows

Row 1 Knit.

Row 2 K3, p24, k3.

Repeat these 2 rows until the piece measures 41" (104cm).

Change to 2 strands of color B held together, and repeat the last 2 rows until the piece measures 30" (76cm) from the color change.

Next 2 rows

Row 1 K1, k2tog, knit to the end—29 stitches.

Row 2 K3, purl to the last 3 stitches, k3.

Repeat these 2 rows 23 more times—6 stitches.

Next 2 rows

Row 1 K1, k2tog, knit to the end—5 stitches.

Row 2 Knit.

Repeat these 2 rows twice more—3 stitches.

Next row K3tog.

Fasten off.

FINISHING

Use a tapestry needle to weave in all the loose ends.

Resist

Hold a marble, golfball, or other resist object on the wrong side of the work, and secure a rubber band around the resist from the right side of the work. Space the resists without particular concern for even spacing or a regular rhythm. Sporadic and spontaneous placement looks great!

Felting

Please refer to the guidelines for *washing machine felting* on page 118.

Once the felting cycle is done, allow the piece to air dry with the resist inside the fabric. Remove the resist after the piece is totally dry. Carefully use scissors to cut the rubber bands, if necessary. Of course, if you use scissors, be mindful not to cut the fabric. Work slowly with very sharp, pointed scissors. (I use fingernail scissors.)

When a pattern calls for "yarn held double throughout," and your yarn is in skein form, try this technique for winding out a perfect double-stranded ball. Place the opened skein around a chair. Snip off the ties binding the fiber. Find both ends of the skein (they will likely be tied together) and hold together. Wrap into a ball by pulling from each end simultaneously. One strand will pull from the left, one will pull from the right, but both will come together if you wrap slowly and patiently. One of the great benefits of this technique is your yarn will be divided perfectly in half.

wood grain scarf

Based on a classic Japanese technique known as mokume,

the Wood Grain Scarf is an exercise in shibori perfection.

Knit in a simple meditative stockinette stitch

with a garter stitch border,

magic happens with basic gathering pleats

that are sewn into the finished knit

prior to felting.

The memory of the pleats remains in the scarf

after it has been felted and the pleating stitches have been

removed. What results is an organic and wonderfully

vibrant fabric that is reminiscent of natural wood, and is

simultaneously urban and edgy.

Level Easy

Knitted Measurements

Before felting

80" x 7" (203cm x 18cm)

After felting

48" x 7" (122cm x 18cm)

Materials

Felting fiber

2 skeins Alchemy Yarns Haiku, 60% mohair, 40% silk, 7/8 oz (25g), 325 yds (297m), 58m Joshua Tree, (**2**) fine

Knitting needles in size US 9 (5.5mm) or size needed to obtain gauge

Waste cotton, silk, or nylon thread (the waste thread must not be made of a felting fiber)

Tapestry needle

Gauge

16 stitches and 20 rows = 4" (10cm) in stockinette stitch with yarn held double, before felting

Notes

The pleats are sewn after the scarf is knit and before it is felted.

Yarn is held double throughout. Please refer to the sidebar on page 27 for detailed instructions on easy winding of a double-stranded skein.

I recommend dry cleaning for the finished piece to keep the resist shape intact.

SCARF

Using 2 strands of yarn held together, cast on 30 stitches. Work in garter stitch (knit every row) for 10 rows.

Next 2 rows

Row 1 (Right Side) Knit.

Row 2 K3, p24, k3.

Repeat these two rows until the scarf measures 78" (198cm).

Work in garter stitch for 10 rows, then bind off all stitches.

FINISHING

Use a tapestry needle to weave in all the loose ends, being sure to weave at least 3" (7.5cm) of each end to ensure a tight hold during the felting process.

Wood grain pleat

Using a tapestry needle threaded with waste yarn, and beginning at one end of the scarf, just inside the garter stitch border, weave the needle in and out along the length of the scarf every ½" (1.25cm) or so, gathering the fabric as you go. Secure the thread tightly with several knots at each end of the scarf. Make a second gathering pleat parallel to the first pleat on the other side of the scarf. The irregularity of sewing by hand will give a great dimension to the gathers and will enhance the wood grain effect. Make sure the pleats are held tightly, so that they will not come undone in the washing machine.

Felting

Please refer to the guidelines for *washing machine felting* on page 118.

Once the felting cycle is done, allow the piece to dry with the pleats intact. Remove the waste yarn carefully after the piece is completely dry.

wine lover's scarf

Wine is a way of life in Northern California—
I drive through vineyards in my neighborhood daily
and marvel at the beauty the glorious grape brings
to the landscape. Whether it be the dynamic colors
of "crush" in the fall harvest or the stunning green
geometric patterns the vine makes in early spring,
the bounty of the grape is sensational
all year long.

Perhaps in hope of remembering the wine—
or, more specifically, the experience associated with
sharing a lovely bottle of wine—I save corks.
When thinking about an interesting resist that would
bring a curious dimension to shibori, I remembered
the burgeoning bag of corks gathered in my kitchen.
The barrel shape of the cork makes for a fascinating
shape in the felted fabric.
And since shibori is "memory in fiber,"
it's a satisfying experience to incorporate the wine
experience into the knitting process!
The center section of the scarf is pleated before felting
for a satisfying texture to rest comfortably against
the back of the neck.

Level Easy

Knitted Measurements

Before felting

Width 18" (46cm)

Length 54" (137cm)

After felting

Width 4" (10cm) at back neck, 12" (30cm) at widest point

Length 44" (112cm)

Materials

Felting fiber

4 skeins of Alchemy Yarns Haiku, 60% mohair, 40% silk, 7/8 oz (25g), 325 yds (297m), 71f Rich Berry, (2) fine

Knitting needles in size US 9 (5.5) or size needed to obtain gauge

Approximately 65 rubber bands

Approximately 65 wine corks (you may substitute foam hair curlers, if desired)

Tapestry needle

Waste cotton or silk yarn

Gauge

16 stitches and 20 rows = 4" (10cm) in stockinette stitch using 2 strands of felting fiber held together (before felting measurement)

Notes

Gauge is not critical for this garment.

Yarn is worked double throughout. Please refer to the sidebar on page 27 for detailed instructions on easy winding of a double-stranded skein.

I recommend dry cleaning for finished piece to keep the resist shape intact.

SCARF

Using 2 strands of yarn held together, cast on 76 stitches, and knit 6 rows.

Next 2 rows

Row 1 (Right Side) Knit.

Row 2 K3, p70, k3.

Repeat these 2 rows until the piece measures 53" (135cm), ending after a wrong-side row.

Knit 6 rows. Bind off all stitches.

FINISHING

Use a tapestry needle to weave in all the loose ends, being sure to weave at least 3" (7.5cm) of each end to ensure a tight hold during the felting process.

Mark neck

Measure 23" (59cm) from one end and place a marker. Repeat on the other end of the scarf.

Note: The center 8" (20cm) will be pleated, rather than have resists set in.

RESIST

Beginning at one end of the scarf, hold a wine cork or other resist object on the wrong side of the work, and secure a rubber band around the resist tightly from the right side of the work. Be sure to loop the rubber band multiple times around the object, in order to hold the resist securely. Space the resists evenly across the width of the scarf (I used 5 or 6 in each "row" of resists), and continue in this manner until you reach the marker. Repeat for the other side.

PLEATING

Beginning at left side of the section marked for pleating, make small gathers in the fabric, approximately ¼" (1cm) in width. Allow the gathers to fold on themselves, like accordion pleats. Using a tapestry needle threaded with waste

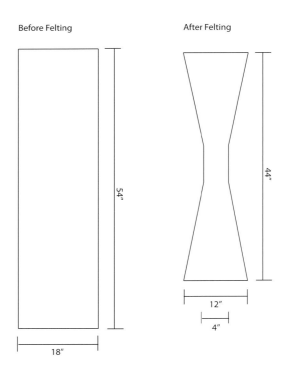

Before Felting

54"

18"

After Felting

44"

12"

4"

cotton or silk yarn (it must be nonfelting yarn), weave the needle through the pleats, gathering the fabric as you go. Secure the waste thread tightly with several knots. Make two more pleats in this manner, evenly spaced in the center section of the scarf, and stopping at the right side stitch marker. The irregularity of sewing by hand will give a great dimension to the gathers. Make sure the pleats are fastened securely, so they will not come undone in the washing machine.

FELTING

Please refer to the guidelines for *washing machine felting* on page 118.

Once the felting cycle is done, allow the piece to air dry with the resist inside the fabric. Remove the resist and waste yarn after the piece is completely dry. Carefully remove the rubber bands and waste yarn, using scissors to cut them, and being mindful not to cut the fabric.

An organism's ability to store, retain, and subsequently recall information is the psychological definition of memory. For our species, memory has a tremendous influence on how we experience life. Whether sensory, long-term, or short-term memory, we form and retrieve memories, and they inform our past, present, and future.

In shibori, there is opportunity to achieve memory in knitting. After you knit the simple Wine Lover's Scarf, you add the wine cork resists to the fabric. You felt the scarf. You remove the corks once the piece is dry. But the scarf remembers the corks. The scarf retains the shape of the cork, even after the resist is removed. When you wear the scarf, you might remember the people with whom you shared the bottle of wine, or the event that was toasted with the bottle of champagne—the corks hold a memory for you, too. Just as our experiences help determine and inform who we are, so does the act of shibori shape and affect knitting.

koi bag

Having been trained as a sculptor,

I am perpetually interested in creating

three-dimensional design in knitwear.

The opportunity to synthesize

embroidery, beads, and optical illusions of

scales and fins was irresistible

when I designed this bag,

and I found myself delightfully challenged

by the prospect of using short rows to

simulate motion and dimension.

What results is a design that is a textural delight

to make and provides a whimsical

and functional piece.

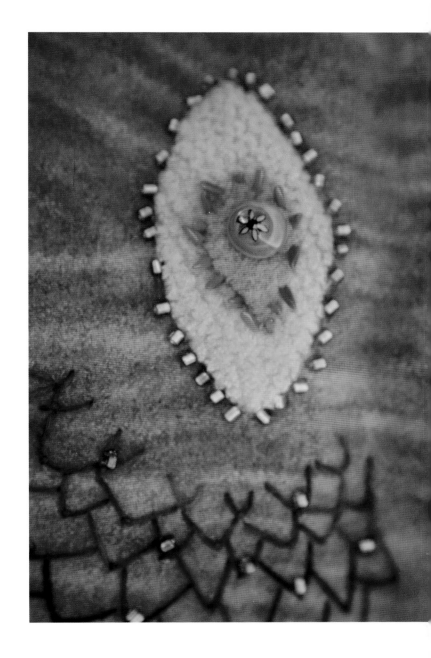

Level Experienced

Knitted measurements

Before felting

Length: 29" (74cm)

Height at the tallest point: 13" (33cm)

Tail width: 11" (28cm)

After felting

Length: 22" (56cm)

Height at the tallest point: 10½" (26.5cm)

Tail width: 9" (23cm)

Materials

Felting fiber

5 skeins of Alchemy Yarns Sanctuary, 70% merino, 30% silk, 1¾ oz (50g), 125 yds (114m), 45c koi pond (color A), (3) light

1 skein each of Alchemy Yarns Sanctuary, 70% merino, 30% silk, 1¾ oz (50g), 125 yds (114m), 5f Persimmon (color B) and 71f Rich Berry (color C), (3) light

Nonfelting fiber

1 skein Alchemy Yarns Bamboo, 100% bamboo, 1¾ oz (50g), 138 yds (126m), 25c Aubergine (color D), (3) light

Knitting needles in size US 6 (4mm) or size needed to obtain gauge

Stitch holder

65 round 5mm beads in turquoise; 16 cylindrical beads, approximately 10mm long in red; and 16 round beads, 16 mm in coordinating colors

Large button for the center of the eye (approximately ⅝" [15mm] in diameter)

Beading needle and thread

Sewing needle and invisible thread (beading thread works well)

4 snaps (shown) or a 12" (30cm) zipper (or other closure for the top of the bag)

Darning needle

Tapestry needle

Gauge

24 stitches and 28 rows = 4" (10cm) in stockinette stitch using color A before felting

Notes

I used a Moving Mud hand-blown glass button for the center of the eye and round beads and cylindrical beads (available from many craft or bead stores) for the embellishment of the eye and the fins. I used a series of 16 larger hand-painted beads along the handle to simulate the bubbles from the fish's mouth.

Short rows are worked in order to create the illusion of a moving fish. The wrap and turn is the key to working successful short rows.

The embroidery, eye panels, beading, handle, and closure are worked after felting.

You can substitute embroidery floss or any other contrasting fiber for the bamboo fiber (color D). Only a few yards of colors B and C are needed. You can substitute any good felting fiber for these colors.

Special Technique

Wrap and Turn

Bring the yarn to the back of work, slip 1 stitch purlwise from the left-hand needle to the right-hand needle, bring the yarn to the front, slip the wrapped stitch back to the left-hand needle again, turn the work around, bring the yarn in position for the next stitch, and work to the end of the row.

FRONT

Tail Fin Part I

*Using color A, cast on 2 stitches and work 2 rows in stockinette stitch.

Next 6 rows

Row 1 (Right Side) Kfb twice—4 stitches.

Row 2 Purl.

Row 3 K1, kfb, kfb, k1—6 stitches.

Row 4 Purl.

Row 5 K1, kfb, knit to the last 2 stitches, kfb, k1—8 stitches.

Row 6 Purl.

Repeat the last 2 rows until you have 22 stitches, ending on a wrong-side row.*

Next 4 rows

Row 1 (Right Side) Knit to the last 2 stitches, kfb, k1—23 stitches.

Row 2 Purl.

Row 3 K1, kfb, knit to the last 2 stitches, kfb, k1—25 stitches.

Row 4 Purl.

Repeat the last 4 rows once more—28 stitches.

Work in stockinette stitch until the piece measures 6" (15.25cm).

Cut the yarn, and place all stitches on a holder.

Tail Fin Part II

Work the same as Tail Fin Part I from * to *.

Next 4 rows

Row 1 (Right Side) K1, kfb, knit to the end—23 stitches.

Row 2 Purl.

Row 3 K1, kfb, knit to the last 2 stitches, kfb, k1—25 stitches.

Row 4 Purl.

Repeat the last 4 rows once more—28 stitches.

Work in stockinette stitch until the piece measures 6" (15cm).

Join Fin

Knit across 28 stitches from the needle, then 28 stitches from the holder—76 stitches.**

Next 2 rows (short rows)

Row 1 (Wrong Side) P29, wrap and turn.

Row 2 Knit.

Repeat these 2 rows 6 more times, purling 1 more stitch before the wrap and turn each time. On the last repeat, you will purl 35 stitches before the wrap and turn.

Next 2 rows

Row 1 (Wrong Side) P1, p2tog, purl to the last 3 stitches, p2tog, p1.

Row 2 Knit.

Repeat these 2 rows until you have 40 stitches left, then purl 1 row.

Next 5 rows

Rows 1 and 2 Bind off 3 stitches, then work to end—34 stitches.

Rows 3 and 4 Bind off 2 stitches, then work to end—30 stitches.

Row 5 Knit.

Body

Next 2 rows (short rows)

Row 1 (Wrong Side) P21, wrap and turn.

Row 2 Knit to the last 2 stitches, kfb, k1.

Repeat these 2 rows 7 more times, purling 2 more stitches before the wrap and turn each time. On the last repeat, you will purl 35 stitches before the wrap and turn.

Next 6 rows

Row 1 (Wrong Side) Purl.

Row 2 Knit to the last 2 stitches, kfb, k1.

Row 3 Purl.

Row 4 Knit to the last 2 stitches, kfb, k1.

Row 5 Purl.

Row 6 K1, kfb, knit to the last 2 stitches, kfb, k1.

Repeat these 6 rows until you have 58 stitches, ending on a right-side row.

Next 6 rows

Rows 1–5 Work in stockinette stitch.

Row 6 K1, kfb, knit to the last 2 stitches, kfb, k1.

Repeat these 6 rows until you have 72 stitches, ending on a right-side row.

Work even in stockinette stitch for 10 rows.

Next 2 rows (short rows)

Row 1 (Wrong Side) P21, wrap and turn.

Row 2 Knit.

Repeat these 2 rows 7 more times, purling 2 more stitches before the wrap and turn each time. On the last repeat, you will purl 35 stitches before the wrap and turn.

Head

Next 2 rows

Row 1 (Wrong Side) Purl.

Row 2 K1, ssk, knit to the last 3 stitches, k2tog, k1.

Repeat these 2 rows until you have 24 stitches left, then purl 1 row.

Next 2 rows

Next row (Right Side) Bind off 12 stitches, knit to the end.

Next row Bind off the remaining 12 stitches.

BACK

Tail Fin

Work the same as Front tail fin to ** (through joining fin), then purl one row.

Next 2 rows (short rows)

Row 1 (Right Side) K29, wrap and turn.

Row 2 Purl.

Repeat these 2 rows 6 more times, knitting 1 more stitch before the wrap and turn each time. On the last repeat, you will knit 35 stitches before the wrap and turn.

Next 2 rows

Row 1 (Wrong Side) K1, ssk, knit to the last 3 stitches, k2tog, k1.

Row 2 Purl.

Repeat these 2 rows until you have 40 stitches left, then knit 1 row.

Next 5 rows

Rows 1 and 2 Bind off 3 stitches, then work to end—34 stitches.

Rows 3 and 4 Bind off 2 stitches, then work to end—30 stitches.

Row 5 Purl.

Body

Next 2 rows (short rows)

Row 1 (Right Side) K1, kfb, k19, wrap and turn.

Row 2 Purl.

Repeat these 2 rows 7 more times, knitting 2 more stitches before the wrap and turn each time. On the last repeat, you will knit 35 stitches before the wrap and turn.

Knit 1 row.

Next 6 rows

Row 1 (Wrong Side) Purl.

Row 2 K1, kfb, knit to the end.

Row 3 Purl.

Row 4 K1, kfb, knit to the end.

Row 5 Purl.

Row 6 K1, kfb, knit to the last 2 stitches, kfb, k1.

Next 6 rows

Rows 1–5 Work in stockinette stitch.

Row 6 K1, kfb, knit to the last 2 stitches, kfb, k1.

Repeat these 6 rows until you have 72 stitches, ending on a right-side row.

Work even in stockinette stitch for 9 rows.

Next 2 rows (short rows)

Row 1 (Right Side) K21, wrap and turn.

Row 2 Purl.

Repeat these 2 rows 7 more times, knitting 2 more stitches before the wrap and turn each time. On the last repeat, you will knit 35 stitches before the wrap and turn.

Head

Knit 1 row.

Next 2 rows

Row 1 (Wrong Side) Purl.

Row 2 K1, ssk, knit to the last 3 stitches, k2tog, k1.

Repeat these 2 rows until you have 24 stitches left, then purl 1 row.

Next 2 rows

Next row (Right Side) Bind off 12 stitches, knit to the end.

Next row Bind off the remaining 12 stitches.

EYE PANELS

Using color B, cast on 20 stitches.

Work 20 rows in garter stitch, then bind off all stitches.

Using color C, cast on 10 stitches.

Work 10 rows in stockinette stitch, then bind off all stitches.

FINISHING

Use a cool iron to press the fish panels on the wrong side. Pin the pieces for seaming with the right sides together. Using color A and a tapestry needle, sew the seam of the bag beginning just above the tail, working around the belly of the fish, and ending on top of the head. The opening at the top of the fish should measure approximately 8" (20.5cm) before felting. Use a tapestry needle to weave in all the loose ends, being sure to weave at least 3" (7.5cm) of each end to ensure a tight hold during the felting process.

Felting

Please refer to the guidelines for *washing machine felting* on page 118.

Felt the individual squares of colors B and C along with the bag before sewing them on.

Allow all the pieces to air dry completely before assembling.

Eye

Note: Instructions are given to make an eye on one side only, for ease of carrying bag.

Make a paper template as follows: draw an oval, measuring approximately 2" × 4" (5cm × 10cm) on a piece of paper for the bottom piece of the eye. Cut it out, and lay the paper template on the bag. Trim the shape as desired, and when you are satisfied with the shape, pin the template on top of the felted color B Eye Panel. Using sharp scissors, cut out the shape.

Repeat this procedure for the top section of the eye using the felted color C Eye Panel, making this template approximately 1" x 2" (2.5cm x 5cm).

Using sewing needle and thread, attach color B Eye Panel to the bag, followed by color C Eye Panel.

Strap

Using color D, cut a strand of yarn 8 yds (7m) long, and fold it in half. You now have a double-thickness strand 4 yds (3.5m) long. Have a helper hold one end of the strand while you hold the other end, each of you twisting the strand to the right. Allow the strand to tighten significantly. When ready, carefully bring the two ends together and allow the strands to twist together, forming a twisted cord. Tie a knot with the two ends that were brought together.

Thread one end of the strap through a darning needle, then insert the needle from the inside of the bag at the top of the tail and secure the strap with a firm double knot. Once the strap is outside of bag, thread the bubble beads (if desired), then bring the needle down through the bag at the top of the mouth, and secure on the inside of the bag, knotting carefully.

Embroidery

Use color D and a darning needle to embroider scales. Begin approximately 1" (2.5cm) to the right of the eye and about 1" (2.5cm) below the top of the bag. Follow the photograph for approximate stitch placement. The stitch used is based on a classic embroidery stitch called the double featherstitch (please check a reference guide for embroidery instruction, or invent your own technique). Allow the stitches to grow a bit longer toward the back of the fish.

Embroider the Tail Fin as well, as shown.

Beading

Using beading needle and thread, sew the beads as desired on the side and tail fins. Follow the photograph for inspiration. Embellish the eye as shown in the photograph, or as desired. The large button works well as the iris for the fish, giving it personality.

When my dad was growing up in the Depression Era in rural Tennessee, he saw fish rain from the sky. He was walking down the sidewalk and started noticing tiny shimmers of silver all over the path in front of him. He reached down to investigate, and picked up a fish. It was still alive. Though a relatively rare meteorological phenomenon, animals can rain from the sky. The most frequently "rained" species are fish, followed by frogs and birds. This remarkable occurrence is usually associated with thunderstorms, when whirlwinds are at play; the winds pick up "debris," which can be carried, animal form intact, for many miles, dropping them off unexpectedly and out of context!

Shibori Creativity explores the harmonious blending of felting and nonfelting fibers, as seen in the Beaded Ruffle Bag (page 50), the Shibori Fez (page 72), and the Poet's Shawl (page 76).

shibori *creativity*

Little Bear's Bonnet and Booty Set **46**

Beaded Ruffle Bag **50**

Whole Heart Baby Sling **54**

Scarf de Triumphe **60**

Op Art Belt **64**

Ska Hat **68**

Shibori Fez **72**

Poet's Shawl **76**

experiments in unlikely combinations of fiber

shibori *creativity*

experiments in unlikely combinations of fiber

While Chapter 1 focuses on simple resist felting, Chapter 2 introduces a whole new method of shibori creativity. The collected patterns incorporate techniques normally not associated with felted knitting, such as slipped stitches and Fair Isle. The focus of this chapter is on a sophisticated interplay of color and texture, along with the exploration of a range of moods from whimsical and flirtatious to contemplative and heroic. This expansive combination of qualities bequeaths a spirit of unbridled creative freedom in these knit designs. Again, the majority of the projects are low-yardage and low-risk, which serves to build your confidence as you go deeper into the exploration of the fascinating opportunities that shibori knitting provides.

Metaphorically, this chapter is about celebrating diversity and richness, and the thrill in watching life's adventure unfold. It's about taking action, making changes, and being courageous. It's also about another kind of letting go. Many of us have grown up hearing the old adage, "Leap and the net will appear," as a way to express faith and hopefulness. I prefer a revision of that statement: "Leap, then leap again."

The longer I live, the more I realize that it's not about waiting for the net to appear. I believe that real transformation happens when we don't get attached to the outcome (the net appearing); rather, the opportunity for change, growth, and challenge comes in the act of leaping.

Focusing primarily on accessories, the projects presented in *Shibori Creativity* reflect an exciting celebration of the many unexpected thrills that shibori knitting offers. Classic Fair Isle and intarsia knitting allows for harmonious blending of felting and nonfelting fibers, included in the projects Scarf de Triumphe (page 60), the Op Art Belt (page 64), and the Ska Hat (page 68). The Shibori Fez (page 72) adds daring new height to the simple slipped stitch technique, creating a finished fabric unlike any other.

May this chapter incite you to bring dramatic color and immense beauty into your everyday life. May you learn to leap, and leap again. And may all the textures and rich terrain of your life be steeped in creativity, satisfaction, and wonderment.

The Op Art Belt (page 64) uses Fair Isle to create a woven effect.

little bear's bonnet and booty set

Wrap that precious little one in

quick-to-knit style and savvy with this set's

unexpected combination of silk bouclé

and the softest French angora.

This is a perfect shower gift or a loving

way to welcome your baby or grand baby.

The shibori element is realized simply and

elegantly in the ruffle,

which can also be omitted to meet personal

preference. The stitch patterns are

wonderful and the softness of the combined

fibers remarkable—all of which makes the

set a timeless heirloom.

Level Intermediate

Knitted Measurements

Bootie length: 4¼" (11cm)

Bootie height: 5" (12.5cm)

Toe depth: 1½" (3.8cm)

Ruffle: 1¼" (3cm)

There is no measurable dimension change after felting the booties.

Bonnet circumference: 15" (38cm)

The bonnet is not felted.

Materials

Felting fiber

1 skein of Alchemy Yarns Furry Kindness, 70% French angora, 30% wool, ⅞ oz (25g), 86 yds (79m), 60a Amethyst (color A), **(3)** light

Nonfelting fiber

1 skein of Alchemy Yarns Pagoda, 100% silk bouclé, 1¼ oz (35.5g), 183 yds (167m), 62c Resolution (color B), **(4)** medium

16" (40cm) circular needle in size US 4 (3.5mm) or size needed to obtain gauge

A set of double-pointed needles in the same size (for ease in constructing the ears)

16" (40cm) circular needle in size US 6 (4mm)

A spare needle in size US 6 (4mm)

Crochet hook in size F-5 (3.75mm)

2 stitch holders

2 shoelaces (to use during felting)

Tapestry needle

Safety pin

Gauge

24 stitches and 28 rows = 4" (10cm) in stockinette stitch with color B and smaller needles

If ever you find yourself in need of a quick ripping out of mohair, angora, or another similarly fuzzy fiber, try this tip: put your knit work in a laundry or Ziploc bag, or other suitable container, and pop it in the freezer. This works best if you leave it overnight, giving time for the yarn to be magically "tamed"! The fibers are not so inclined to fuse together after freezing, and your rip will be a much more pleasant process—or at least frustration-free, if not necessarily a happy occasion!

Notes

Although I recommend felting the booties to bring out the unusual characteristics of the angora fiber, I do not recommend felting the bonnet. The bonnet is made primarily of the silk fiber, and will not be affected by the shibori process.

Once felted, the ruffle at the top of the bootie will fall to the outside of the bootie. Pay particular attention to weaving in your ends, knowing the wrong side will become the right side after felting.

Angora does not felt with the same characteristics as wool or mohair. A shorter time will be needed for felting—approximately 5 minutes on the gentle cycle. The fabric created will still show stitch definition, and the transformation will be a bit more subtle than that of more typical felting fibers. Do not overfelt!

Stitch Patterns

2x2 Rib Pattern

(Worked over a multiple of 4 stitches plus 2)

Row 1 K2, *p2, k2; repeat from * to the end.

Row 2 P2, *k2, p2; repeat from * to the end.

Repeat rows 1 and 2 for 2x2 rib pattern.

1x1 Rib Pattern

(Worked over an even number of stitches)

Every row *K1, p1; repeat from * to the end.

Seed Stitch Pattern

(Worked over an even number of stitches)

Row 1 *K1, p1; repeat from * to the end.

Row 2 *P1, k1; repeat from * to the end.

Repeat rows 1 and 2 for seed stitch pattern.

BOOTIES (MAKE 2)

Ruffle

Using color B and larger circular needle, cast on 68 stitches, and knit 2 rows.

Work 4 rows in stockinette stitch, beginning with a knit row.

Next row K2tog across the row—34 stitches.

Purl one row.

Note: If you want to eliminate the ruffle, cast on 34 stitches, and knit 2 rows.

Cuff

Change to color A, and work 16 rows in 2x2 rib pattern.

Next row (make eyelets) K1, *yo, k2tog; repeat from * to the last stitch, k1.

Purl one row.

Instep

Work in 2x2 rib pattern across 12 stitches, and slip these stitches onto a stitch holder.

Work in 2x2 rib pattern across 10 stitches, and slip the remaining 12 stitches from the left needle onto a second holder.

Working across the center 10 stitches, continue in 2x2 rib pattern for 11 more rows.

Next row (Right Side) Work in 2x2 rib pattern across 10 stitches, then pick up and knit 8 stitches from the side of the instep, then work in 2x2 rib pattern across the 12 stitches from the left-side holder.

Next row (Wrong Side) Work in 2x2 rib pattern across row, pick up and knit 8 stitches from the other side of the instep, then work in 2x2 rib pattern across the 12 stitches from the remaining holder—50 stitches.

Foot

Work 10 rows in 2x2 rib pattern.

Sole

Next 3 rows

Row 1 (Right Side) P2tog, p20, p2tog, p2, p2tog, p20, p2tog—46 stitches.

Row 2 (Wrong Side) Knit.

Next row (Right Side) P2tog, p18, p2tog, p2, p2tog, p18, p2tog—42 stitches.

Divide stitches in half, keeping the first 21 stitches on the original needle, and placing the second 21 stitches on a spare needle.

Bind off. Seam sole using a three-needle bind-off.

Twist Laces for Booties (make 2)

Using color B, measure a strand of yarn 176" (447cm) long, and fold it in 4 equal parts. You now have a quadrupled strand of yarn that is 44" (112cm) long. Have a helper hold one end of the strand while you hold the other end. Both of you should then twist the strand to the right. Allow the strand to tighten significantly. When ready, carefully bring the two ends together and allow the strand to twist together. Tie a knot with the two ends that were brought together and trim any excess as desired.

Do not insert the twist laces into booties before felting!

Finishing

Use a tapestry needle to sew the back seam of the booties.

Weave in all the loose ends, being sure to weave at least 3" (7.5cm) of each end to ensure a tight hold during the felting process.

Weave the shoelaces in and out of the eyelets, and tie securely. The shoelaces will keep the eyelets open during the felting process, so that the twist laces may be inserted after felting and drying.

Felting

Please refer to the guidelines for *washing machine felting* on page 118.

Remove the shoelaces, and insert the twist laces when the booties are fully dry. Tie in a bow on the front or side, as desired.

BONNET

Using color B and the smaller circular needle, cast on 74 stitches, and work four rows in garter stitch.

Work in stockinette stitch until the piece measures 5" (12.5cm) from the beginning.

Bind off 24 stitches at beginning of next two rows—26 stitches.

Continue working in stockinette stitch for 5" (12.5cm) more.

Next row (Right Side) K2tog across the row, binding off all stitches as you go.

Use a tapestry needle to sew the top and side seams.

Neck trim

Using color B and the smaller circular needle and with the right side facing, pick up and knit 52 stitches along the garter stitch edge.

Work in 1x1 rib pattern for 6 rows, and then bind off all stitches in pattern.

Ruffle

Using color A and the larger circular needle and with the right side facing, pick up and knit 70 stitches around the front of the bonnet.

Work four rows in garter stitch, then bind off all stitches.

Using color B and the crochet hook, work two rows of single crochet along the same edge.

Next row (Right Side) Work 2 sc into each stitch.

Repeat this row once more.

Fasten off.

Ears (make 2)

On the seam of the left side of top of bonnet, place a pin 3½" (9cm) from the band at front of bonnet. Using color A and the double-pointed needles, pick up and knit 6 stitches on each side of the safety pin—12 stitches.

Work 6 rows in seed stitch.

Next 2 rows

Row 1 K1, k2tog, work in seed stitch pattern to the last 3 stitches, k2tog, k1.

Row 2 Work in seed stitch pattern.

Repeat these 2 rows until you have 4 stitches left.

Next row K2tog twice—4 stitches.

Knit the remaining 2 stitches together and fasten off.

Using color B and and the crochet hook, work two rounds SC around each ear.

Twist Ties (make 2)

Cut a strand of yarn 160" (406cm) long. Fold the strand into four 40" (101.5cm) lengths. Make these ties using the same technique as used for the bootie twist laces. Use a tapestry needle to attach ties to the angora band at the side of the bonnet.

beaded ruffle bag

This classic bag is a sensational introduction

to shibori and exemplifies the exciting

opportunity to celebrate

the contrasting characteristics of color and

texture in knitting.

A modern silhouette is knit all in felting

fiber, using clever, but simple shaping. The

nonfelting fiber is worked in an exaggerated

ruffle around the top edge,

providing a fun and flirtatious attitude!

Small glass beads bring a subtle sparkle and

dimension to the handle, making this piece

versatile and vivacious.

Level Intermediate

Knitted Measurements

Before felting

Height: 13" (33cm); Base width: 7½" (19cm)

Base circumference: 15" (38cm); Circumference at the widest part: 24" (61cm)

Button tab: 2½" x ⅞" (6.25cm x 2.2cm); Strap: 2¾" x 26" (7cm x 66cm)

After felting

Height: 9" (23cm); Base width: 6½" (16.5cm)

Base circumference: 13" (33cm); Circumference at the widest part: 21" (53.5cm)

Button tab: 2" x ⅞" (5cm x 2.2cm); Strap: 1¾" x 26" (4.5cm x 66cm)

Materials

Felting fiber

3 skeins of Alchemy Yarns Sanctuary, 70% merino, 30% silk, 1¾ oz (50g), 125yds (114m), 05f Persimmon (color A), **(3)** light

Nonfelting fiber

1 skein of Alchemy Yarns Pagoda, 100% silk bouclé, 1¼ oz (35.5g), 183 yds (167m), 49c Punky (color B), **(4)** medium

16" (40cm) circular needle in size US 6 (4mm) or size needed to obtain gauge

A set of double-pointed needles in the same size (for ease in constructing the strap)

Crochet hook in size F-5 (3.75mm)

Stitch markers

1 small button

1 shoelace (to hold the buttonhole open during felting)

Invisible beading thread and beading needle (available in most craft stores)

½ oz (15g) of small rectangular glass beads, tubular shaped, approximately ¼" (6mm) length (Blue Moon's beads in hot pink are shown.)

Tapestry needle

Gauge

20 stitches and 24 rows = 4" (10cm) in garter stitch before felting

Note

Markers are essential for this pattern, for both the right twist and graduated circumference in the design.

Special Stitches

Right twist

Knit the second stitch on the left needle without dropping it off, knit the first stitch, then drop both stitches off.

BASE

Using color A and circular needles, cast on 24 stitches and knit 2 rows.

Next 2 rows

Row 1 (Right Side) K1, kfb, knit to the last 2 stitches, kfb, k1.

Row 2 Knit.

Repeat these 2 rows until you have 36 stitches.

Work evenly in garter stitch (knit every row) for 10 rows.

Next 2 rows

Row 1 (Right Side) K1, ssk, knit to the last 3 stitches, k2tog, k1.

Row 2 Knit.

Repeat these 2 rows until you have 24 stitches.

SIDES

Place a marker on the needle, pick up and knit 16 stitches along the nearest side of the piece, place another marker, pick up and knit 24 stitches along the cast-on edge, place another marker, pick up and knit 16 stitches along the next side of the piece, place another marker (this marker should be a different color or design to denote the beginning of the round)—80 stitches and 4 markers placed.

Join to work in the round by knitting the first of the original 24 stitches, and knit 1 round.

Next 6 rounds

Rounds 1–5 *Right twist, knit to the last 2 stitches before the marker, right twist, sl marker; repeat from * to the beginning of the round.

Round 6 *Right twist, k1, m1, knit to the last 3 stitches before the next marker, m1, k1, right twist twice, knit to the last 2 stitches before the next marker, right twist, sl marker; repeat from * once more to the beginning of the round.

Repeat these 6 rounds until you have 136 stitches.

Work Rounds 1–5 (without any more increases) until the sides measure 13" (33cm).

Work in garter stitch for 6 rounds (knit 1 round, then purl 1 round).

Bind off all stitches.

RUFFLE

Using color B and with the right side facing, pick up and knit 1 stitch in every stitch of the lowest ridge of the garter stitch border at the top of the bag—136 stitches. Join to work in the round by knitting the first stitch that you picked up. Mark that first stitch, and work in stockinette stitch for 5 rounds (knit every round).

Next round Kfb around—272 stitches.

Work in stockinette stitch for 19 rounds.

Bind off all stitches.

Crochet edging Using color B, work 3 rounds of single crochet around the entire ruffle and fasten off.

STRAP

Using color A and a double-pointed needle, and with the wrong side facing, pick up and knit 14 stitches at the top of a "short" side panel.

Work in garter stitch for 25" (63.5cm).

Using color A and a double-pointed needle, pick up and knit 14 stitches on the opposite side of the bag, and join these stitches to the strap using a three-needle bind-off.

BUTTON TAB

Using color A and a double-pointed needle, and with the right side facing, pick up and knit 12 stitches, centered at the top of a "long" side panel.

Work in garter stitch for 6 rows, then bind off all stitches.

BUTTONHOLE TAB

Using color A and a double-pointed needle, pick up and knit 12 stitches on the opposite side of the bag, and knit 2 rows.

Next 2 rows (buttonhole)

Row 1 K5, bind off 2 stitches, k5.

Row 2 K5, cast on 2 stitches, k5.

Knit 2 rows, then bind off all stitches.

FINISHING

Use a tapestry needle to weave in all the loose ends, being sure to weave at least 3" (7.5cm) of each end to ensure a tight hold during the felting process.

Tie a shoelace through the buttonhole to keep it from closing during the felting process.

Felting

Please refer to the guidelines for *washing machine felting* on page 118.

Shape by hand, especially pulling out any areas that might have drawn in more

tightly than desired during the felting process. Allow the bag to air dry gently and slowly, preferably without any undue weight pulling on any part, especially the strap (unless you want a longer strap). With a cool iron, soften the silk (nonfelting) fiber by gently pressing it. Doing this will give the silk great suppleness and will add flounce to the ruffle.

When the bag is completely dry, sew a button to the buttonhole tab.

Bead Embellishment

Using the beading needle and thread, and beginning at one end of the strap, sew 3 to 4 beads per ridge of felted fabric. The beads are meant to fit in the little groove that is created by the garter stitch after felting. Do not try to make the beads line up in perfect rows. A more natural and somewhat irregular placement will bring depth and a good rhythm of color and light to the strap. Do not create unnecessary tension by pulling too tightly on the thread.

whole heart baby sling

Sturdy, soft, and reliable are qualities

associated with felted shibori fabric,

making the technique an ideal match

for creating a unique and

practical baby sling.

Knitting the piece is a great exercise

in simplicity, with the super chunky

yarn working up in a satisfying flash!

Playing with the variation on stitch size

is tremendously fun, and results

in a lacy pattern,

with the sections knit in the lighter-

weight nonfelting fiber spaced

rhythmically between the larger color

panels of felting fiber.

Level Easy

Knitted Measurements

Before felting

Length: 30" (76cm)

Width at the widest part: 24" (61cm)

Width at the shoulder: 7" (18cm)

After felting

Length: 27" (68.5cm)

Width at the widest part: 22" (56cm)

Width at the shoulder: 5½" (14cm)

Materials

Felting fiber

4 skeins of Alchemy Yarns Lux, 70% merino, 30% silk, 3½ oz (100g), 75 yds (68.5m), 21e Green Plum (color A), 🌀 super bulky

2 skeins of Alchemy Yarns Lux, 70% merino, 30% silk, 3½ oz (100g), 75 yds (68.5m), 32e Fig (color C), 🌀 super bulky

Nonfelting fiber

1 skein of Alchemy Yarns Pagoda, 100% silk bouclé, 1¼ oz (35.5g), 183 yds (167m), 64c Hidden Place (color B), 🌀 medium

16" (40cm) knitting needles in size US 11 (8 mm) or size needed to obtain gauge

24" (60cm) circular knitting needles in size US 5 (3.75mm)

Tapestry needle

Gauge

12 stitches and 16 rows = 4" (10cm) in stockinette stitch using felting fiber and the larger needles

Notes

Two sets of needles are used in the piece, one for the heavier-weight fiber, and one for the lighter-weight fiber.

The sling is made in one piece, though the directions designate the front and back for clarity.

FRONT

Using color A and the larger needles, cast on 38 stitches.

Row 1 Kfb, knit to the last stitch, kfb—2 stitches increased.

Row 2 Purl.

Repeat these 2 rows until you have 72 stitches.

Work even in stockinette stitch until the piece measures 6" (15cm), ending with a purl row.

Change to color B and the smaller needles.

Next row (Right Side) Kfb across the row—144 stitches.

Work even in garter stitch for 3 rows.

Change to color C.

Next 2 rows

Row 1 K2tog across the row—72 stitches.

Row 2 Change to the larger needles, and purl.

Work even in stockinette stitch until this color section measures 3½" (9cm), ending with a purl row.

Change to color B and the smaller needles.

Next row (Right Side) Kfb across the row—144 stitches.

Work even in garter stitch for 3 rows.

Change to color A.

Next 4 rows

Row 1 K2tog across the row—72 stitches.

Row 2 Change to the larger needles, and purl.

Row 3 K1, ssk, knit to the last 3 stitches, k2tog, k1—2 stitches decreased.

Row 4 Purl.

Repeat rows 3 and 4 until this color section measures 5" (12.5cm), ending with a purl row.

**Change to color B and the smaller needles.

Next 4 rows

Row 1 Kfb across the row—the number of stitches is doubled.

Row 2 Knit.

Row 3 K1, ssk, knit to the last 3 stitches, k2tog, k1—2 stitches decreased.

Row 4 Knit.**

Change to color C.

Next 4 rows

Row 1 K2tog across the row—the number of stitches is halved.

Row 2 Change to the larger needles, and purl.

Row 3 K1, ssk, knit to the last 3 stitches, k2tog, k1—2 stitches decreased.

Row 4 Purl.

Repeat rows 3 and 4 until this color section measures 2¾" (7cm), ending with a purl row.

Work a color B section from ** to ** (with decreasing).

Change to color A.

Next 4 rows

Row 1 K2tog across the row—the number of stitches is halved.

Row 2 Change to the larger needles, and purl.

Row 3 K1, ssk, knit to the last 3 stitches, k2tog, k1—2 stitches decreased.

Row 4 Purl.

Repeat rows 3 and 4 until this color section measures 4¼" (11cm), ending with a purl row.

Work a color B section from ** to ** (with decreasing).

Change to color C.

Next 4 rows

Row 1 K2tog across the row—the number of stitches is halved.

Row 2 Change to the larger needles, and purl.

Row 3 K1, ssk, knit to the last 3 stitches, k2tog, k1—2 stitches decreased.

Row 4 Purl.

Repeat rows 3 and 4 until you have 20 stitches.

Work even in stockinette stitch until this color section measures 1½" (3.8cm), ending with a purl row.

***Change to color B and the smaller needles.

Next row Kfb across the row—40 stitches.

Work even in garter stitch for 3 rows (no shaping).***

Change to color A.

Next 2 rows

Row 1 K2tog across the row—20 stitches.

Row 2 Change to the larger needles and purl.

Work even in stockinette stitch until this color section measures 4" (10cm), ending with a purl row

Place marker at the edge of the fabric, to denote the top of the piece. If you would like the sling to be longer, work a few more rows in this color section.

BACK

Continue in color A and work even in stockinette stitch until this color section measures 4" (10cm), or same length as front section A, from the marker.

Work a color B section from *** to *** (without shaping).

Change to color C.

Next 4 rows

Row 1 K2tog across the row—20 stitches.

Row 2 Change to the larger needles and purl.

Row 3 Kfb, knit to the last stitch, kfb—2 stitches increased.

Row 4 Purl.

Repeat rows 3 and 4 until this color section measures 1½" (3.8cm), ending with a purl row.

****Change to color B and the smaller needles.

Next 4 rows

Row 1 Kfb across the row—the number of stitches is doubled.

Row 2 Knit.

Row 3 Kfb, knit to the last stitch, kfb—2 stitches increased.

Row 4 Knit.****

Change to color A.

Next 4 rows

Row 1 K2tog across the row—the number of stitches is halved.

Row 2 Change to the larger needles and purl.

Row 3 Kfb, knit to the last stitch, kfb—2 stitches increased.

Row 4 Purl.

Repeat rows 3 and 4 until this color section measures 4¼" (11cm), ending with a purl row.

Work a color B section from **** to **** (with increasing).

Change to color C.

Next 4 rows

Row 1 K2tog across the row—the number of stitches is halved.

Row 2 Change to the larger needles and purl.

Row 3 Kfb, knit to the last stitch, kfb—2 stitches increased.

Row 4 Purl.

Repeat rows 3 and 4 until this color section measures 2¾" (7cm), ending with a purl row.

Work a color B section from **** to **** (with increasing).

Change to color A.

Next 4 rows

Row 1 K2tog across the row—the number of stitches is halved.

Row 2 Change to the larger needles and purl.

Row 3 Kfb, knit to the last stitch, kfb—2 stitches increased.

Row 4 Purl.

Repeat rows 3 and 4 until you have 72 stitches.

Work even in stockinette stitch until this color section measures 5" (12.5cm), ending with a purl row.

Change to color B and the smaller needles.

Next row Kfb across the row—144 stitches.

Work even in garter stitch for 3 rows.

Change to color C.

Next 2 rows

Row 1 K2tog across the row—72 stitches.

Row 2 Change to the larger needles, and purl.

Work even in stockinette stitch until this color section measures 3½" (9cm), ending with a purl row.

Change to color B.

Next row Kfb across the row—36 stitches.

Work even in garter stitch for 3 rows.

Change to color A.

Next 2 rows

Row 1 K2tog across the row—the number of stitches is halved.

Row 2 Change to the larger needles, and purl.

Work even in stockinette stitch until this color section measures 3" (7.5cm), ending with a purl row.

Next 2 rows

Row 1 K1, ssk, knit to the last 3 stitches, k2tog, k1—2 stitches decreased.

Row 2 Purl.

Repeat the last 2 rows until you have 38 stitches.

Bind off all stitches.

EDGING

Sew the bottom edges together.

Using color B with the right side facing, and the smaller needle, pick up and knit approximately 200 stitches around one side of the opening (exact count is not critical).

Join to work in the round by knitting the first stitch that you picked up, and work 4 rounds in garter stitch (knit 1 round, then purl 1 round).

Bind off all stitches.

Work the same for the other opening.

FINISHING

Use a tapestry needle to weave in all the loose ends, being sure to weave at least 3" (7.5cm) of each end to ensure a tight hold during the felting process.

Felting

Please refer to the guidelines for *washing machine felting* on page 118.

Be sure not to overfelt; check the piece every 5 minutes in the gentle cycle.

Shape by hand, especially pulling out any areas that might have drawn in more tightly than desired during the felting process. Allow the sling to air dry completely before use.

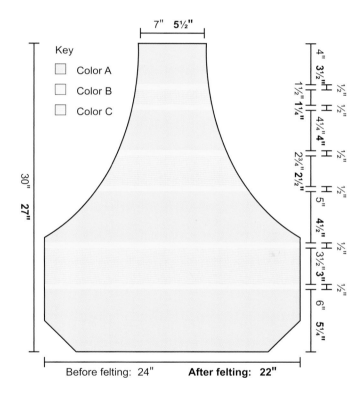

Key
☐ Color A
☐ Color B
☐ Color C

7" 5½"

30" 27"

4" 3½" ½" ½"
1½" 1¼" 4¼" 4" ½"
2¾" 2½" ½"
5" ½"
4½" ½"
3½" 3" ½"
6" 5¼"

Before felting: 24"   **After felting: 22"**

scarf de triumphe

The deeper I dig into the realm of knit shibori, the more fascinated I become by the opportunity to create really unique finished fabric. Garter stitch, of all simple things, takes my breath away when felted—particularly in the merino/silk blend shown in this piece. Something about this texture reminds me of corrugated cardboard—certainly, not the way I feel about cardboard as an adult, but with the love, respect, and beautiful reverence I had for the material as a kid, when a big empty box provided untold excitement and opportunity for imaginative exploration.

Scarf de Triumphe presents a spectacular knit experience. The garter stitch does its beautiful and uncomplicated thing while a simple intarsia technique brings a unique dimension to the work. Combining felting and nonfelting fiber in an easy-to-memorize circle motif makes the piece a relaxing knit.

The felted fabric that results is something unlike any other knit garment I have experienced. The nonfelting fiber windows are like little confessionals; light filters through the shibori fabric, and something truly original and special happens in the blending of subtle color and deeply satisfying texture.

Level Intermediate

Knitted Measurements

Before felting

7" x 67" (18cm x 170cm) including the fringe

After felting

5" x 79" (12.5cm x 200cm) including the fringe

Materials

Felting fiber

2 skeins each of Alchemy Yarns Sanctuary, 70% merino, 30% silk, 1¾ oz (50g), 125yds (114m), 35e Fauna (color A) and 96e Two Rock (color B), (3) light

Nonfelting fiber

1 skein each of Alchemy Yarns Pagoda, 100% silk bouclé, 1¼ oz (35.5g), 183 yds (167m), 96e Two Rock (color C) and 84m Fieldstone (color D), (4) medium

16" (40cm) circular needle in size US 6 (4mm) or size needed to obtain gauge

A set of double-pointed needles in the same size

Stitch markers

Tapestry needle

Gauge

20 stitches and 34 rows = 4" (10cm) in garter stitch before felting

Notes

Six blocks are made, three in each base color. All blocks are worked together.

The scarf is worked using intarsia, with five strands of yarn in play each time the ovals are made. No strands are carried behind the work.

It is helpful to work with manageable lengths of fiber in each intarsia section. To ensure maximum use of your fiber's yardage, I recommend cutting strands of the fibers for those sections as follows: for colors A and B, cut strands approximately 100" (254cm) long; for colors C and D, cut strands approximately 110" (279.5cm) long.

Always keep the full ball of color A or B in play at the right-hand edge of the scarf. This yarn is used to work the garter rows in between the intarsia motifs. This will leave fewer ends to weave in later.

The ovals are always worked in stockinette stitch, while the background is worked in garter stitch.

BEGINNING FRINGE AND EDGING

Using color A and a double-pointed needle, cast on 3 stitches. Work an I-cord (see glossary, page 121) 6" (15cm) long and place this piece on a spare needle. Make 3 more I-cords that measure approximately 4" (10cm), 5½" (14cm), and 6½" (16.5cm). Place the cords on the circular needle in the order in which they are listed above and as shown in photograph.

Next row Using color A, k3 stitches of the first I-cord, *cast on 8 stitches, k3 stitches of the next I-cord; repeat from * twice more—36 stitches.

Knit 2 rows.

*Change to color B, and knit 2 rows. Change to color A, and knit 2 rows; repeat from * once more.

Change to color B, and knit 2 rows.

Change to color A, and knit 4 rows.

SCARF BLOCK 1

Using color A, knit 6 rows. Then work intarsia chart using colors A and C.

*Using color A, knit 12 rows, then work chart; repeat from * once more.

Using color A, knit 6 rows.

SCARF BLOCK 2

Change to color B, and knit 6 rows. Then work intarsia chart using colors B and D.

*Using color B, knit 12 rows, then work chart; repeat from * once more.

Using color B, knit 6 rows.

SCARF BLOCKS 3 & 5

Work the same as Scarf Block 1.

SCARF BLOCKS 4 & 6

Work the same as Scarf Block 2.

ENDING EDGING AND FRINGE

Using color B, knit 4 rows.

*Change to color A, and knit 2 rows. Change to color B, and knit 2 rows; repeat from * once more.

Change to color A, and knit 2 rows

Change to color B, and knit 3 rows.

Next row Work an I-cord 6" (15cm) long using the first 3 stitches of the row. Bind off these stitches and reattach yarn to the remaining 33 stitches on the left-hand needle.

Bind off the next 8 stitches.

Work an I-cord 4½" (11.5cm) long using the next 3 stitches. Bind off these stitches and reattach yarn to the remaining 22 stitches on the left-hand needle.

Bind off the next 8 stitches.

Work an I-cord 5" (12.5cm) long using the next 3 stitches. Bind off these stitches and reattach yarn to the remaining 11 stitches.

Bind off the next 8 stitches.

Work an I-cord 6½" (16.5cm) long using the last 3 stitches. Bind off.

FINISHING

Use a tapestry needle to weave in all the loose ends, being sure to weave at least 3" (7.5cm) of each end to ensure a tight hold during the felting process.

Felting

Please refer to the guidelines for *washing machine felting* on page 118.

Shape by hand, pulling out any areas that might have drawn in more tightly than desired during the felting process. Allow the scarf to air dry gently and slowly. Block lightly to size if needed. The silk of the Pagoda fiber responds beautifully to an iron and softens tremendously when ironed at a rather cool setting.

When I was a kid, my dad gave me a little pocketknife and a giant cardboard box he found behind an appliance store. With these tools, I built the mother of all playhouses—an arched doorway, windows on each wall that opened and closed, a duct-taped pitched roof, and makeshift curtains sloppily sewn from outgrown clothes. Little paintings adorned each wall, due mostly to the fact that I was so intrigued by the effects I could get with crayon on cardboard.

That deeply satisfying saturation of color and texture stays with me all these years later, and finds its way into the Scarf de Triumphe. Memories of simple things that happen to us long ago bring depth and dimension, to both our knits and our lives.

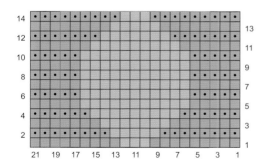

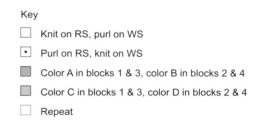

Key

- ☐ Knit on RS, purl on WS
- ⊡ Purl on RS, knit on WS
- Color A in blocks 1 & 3, color B in blocks 2 & 4
- Color C in blocks 1 & 3, color D in blocks 2 & 4
- Repeat

op art belt

Optical illusions are intriguing for knitters.

They are fun to knit and their patterns are

generally easy to memorize.

Optical illusions also provide a great opportunity

for playing with simple color contrasts.

This belt incorporates both a felting

and a nonfelting fiber,

so the optical illusion is even greater,

given the natural tendencies of the fibers used.

The nonfelting fiber has the luster of silk,

while the felting fiber gives a more matte finish.

Level Intermediate

Knitted Measurements

Measurements are given for XS (S, M, L, XL) sizes in that order

Before felting

4½" for all sizes including hem x 28 (32, 36, 40, 44)"
(11.5cm x 71 [81, 91, 101.5, 112]cm)

After felting

3½" for all sizes including hem x 26 (30, 34, 38, 40)"
(9cm x 66 [76, 86, 96.5, 101.5]cm)

Materials

Felting fiber

1 (2, 2, 2, 3) skeins of Alchemy Yarns Sanctuary, 70% merino, 30% silk, 1¾ oz (50g), 125 yds (114m), 06f Poppy (color A), (3) light

Nonfelting fiber

1 skein of Alchemy Yarns Silk Purse, 100% silk, 1¾ oz (50g), 138 yds (126m), 89c Black & Blue (color B), (3) light

28" (70cm) circular needle in size US 6 (4mm) or size needed to obtain gauge

2 large snaps or closures of your choice, 1½" (3.8cm) in diameter

Sewing thread to match color A

Tapestry needle

Gauge

24 stitches and 28 rows = 4" (10cm) in chart pattern before felting

Notes

Work with short strands of color B (approximately 8 yds [7.3m]) to avoid tangling the two fibers used in the Fair Isle pattern. Simply pull color B free from color A after every few rows of knitting to keep knots from forming in the yarn that is carried.

Weaving in the ends as you go will save a great deal of time when the piece is completed.

The pattern repeat is 24 stitches wide, which equals 4" (10cm) before felting. To make the belt larger or smaller, add or subtract multiples of 24 stitches as desired. The snaps may be sewn anywhere, creating more flexibility in the fit, which allows you to wear the belt high at the natural waist or low at the hip.

When choosing a size, allow approximately 3" (7.5cm) for overlap at the snap closure.

BOTTOM HEM

Using color A, cast on 168 (192, 216, 240, 264) stitches, and knit 2 rows to form hem.

BELT

Work sections A and B of the chart in Fair Isle, then work section A again. Be sure to carry the color not in use across the wrong side. The chart will be repeated 7 (8, 9, 10, 11) times across.

Using color A, knit 2 rows.

TOP HEM

Using color A, purl 2 rows to form hem.

Bind off all stitches.

FINISHING

Using color A and a tapestry needle, sew the hems to the wrong side.

Use a darning needle to weave in all the loose ends, being sure to weave at least 3" (7.5cm) of each end to ensure a tight hold during the felting process.

Felting

Please refer to the guidelines for *washing machine felting* on page 118. Pull fabric into shape, because some areas of the belt may have pulled in more tightly than others.

When the belt is fully dry, try it on to position the snaps. Using sewing thread, sew the snaps or closures in place.

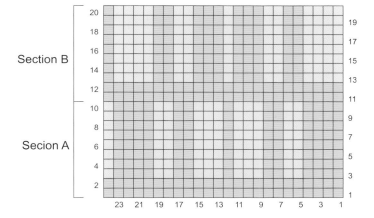

Section B

Secion A

Key

☐ Knit on RS, purl on WS

▨ Color A

☐ Color B

ska hat

This funky fedora is reminiscent of the pork pie hat

made popular by ska bands of the 1980s.

Rich with style and savvy,

the unisex fedora incorporates an unusual

top-down knit, as well as a right-twist stitch that

shows incredible stitch definition—

a rarity in felted fabrics.

The Fair Isle hatband pays homage to the great

bands of the era—The English Beat, The Specials,

and with a special nod to The Clash—

with its telltale hipster diamond motif.

For best results, choose high contrast colors

for the hatband to ensure the

most striking appearance.

Level Intermediate

Knitted Measurements

Before felting

Top of crown: 6" x 6½" (15cm x 16.5cm)

Height: 6½" (16.5cm)

Circumference at the base: 24" (61cm)

Circumference at the widest part of the brim: 28" (71cm)

Brim depth from the garter ridges: 4½" (11.5cm)

Hat band: 3" x 27" (7.5cm x 68.5cm)

After felting

Top of crown: 4½" x 6" (11.5cm x 15cm)

Height: 5" (12.5cm)

Circumference at the base: 22" (56cm)

Circumference at the widest part of the brim: 27" (68.5cm)

Brim depth from the garter ridges: 3" (7.5cm)

Hat band: 2½" x 24" (6.5cm x 61cm)

Materials

Felting fiber

3 skeins of Alchemy Yarns Sanctuary, 70% merino, 30% silk, 1¾ oz (50g), 125 yds (114m), 92w Moonstone (color A), (3) light

1 skein of Alchemy Yarns Sanctuary, 70% merino, 30% silk, 1¾ oz (50g), 125 yds (114m),12w Ocean Floor (color B), (3) light

Nonfelting fiber

1 skein of Alchemy Yarns Pagoda, 100% silk bouclé, 1¼ oz (35.5g), 183 yds (167m), 42m Silver (color C), (4) medium

16" (40cm) circular needle in size US 6 (4mm) or size needed to obtain gauge.

Stitch markers

Tapestry needle

Sewing needle and thread to match color B

Gauge

20 stitches and 24 rows = 4" (10cm) in garter stitch before felting

24 stitches and 28 rows = 4" (10cm) in Ska Diamond pattern (see chart)

Notes

The hat is knit from the top down.

Markers will be your best friends on this pattern. Use them for placement of the right twist and for the graduated circumference in the design.

Special Stitch

Right twist—knit the second stitch on the left-hand needle without dropping it off, then knit the first stitch on the left-hand needle, then drop both stitches off.

CROWN

Using color A, cast on 14 stitches, and knit 2 rows.

Next 2 rows

Row 1 (Right Side) K1, kfb, knit to the last 2 stitches, kfb, k1.

Row 2 Knit.

Repeat these 2 rows until you have 30 stitches.

Work evenly in garter stitch for 36 rows.

Next 2 rows

Row 1 (Right Side) K1, ssk, knit to the last 3 stitches, k2tog, k1.

Row 2 Knit.

Repeat these 2 rows until you have 14 stitches left.

SIDES

Place a marker on the needle (pl m), pick up and knit 32 stitches down the nearest side of the piece, place another marker on the needle, pick up and knit 14 stitches across the cast-on edge, place another marker on the needle, pick up and knit 32 stitches up the next side of the piece, place another marker on the needle (this marker should be in a different color or design to denote the beginning of the round)—92 stitches and 4 markers placed.

Join to work in the round by knitting the 1st stitch on the left-hand needle, and knit 1 round.

Next 6 rounds

Rounds 1–5 *Knit to the next marker, slip marker (sl m), right twist, knit to 2 stitches before the next marker, right twist, sl m; repeat from * once more.

Round 6 *Kfb, knit to the last stitch before the marker, kfb, sl m, right twist, knit to 2 stitches before the next marker, right twist, sl m; repeat from * once more.

Repeat these 6 rounds until you have 120 stitches.

Remove all the markers, except the one that denotes the beginning of the round.

Work in garter stitch for 4 rounds (knit 1 round, then purl 1 round.)

BRIM

Set up round *K20, pl m; repeat from * 4 times more, k to the end.

Next round *Knit to the last stitch before the marker, m1, k1, m1; repeat from * to the end—132 stitches.

Work in stockinette stitch for 5 rounds (knit every round.)

Next round *Knit to the last stitch before the marker, m1, k1, m1; repeat from * to the end—144 stitches.

Work evenly in stockinette stitch until the brim measures 4½" (11.5cm) from the garter ridges at the base of hat.

Next round Purl to form the turning ridge for hem.

Work in stockinette stitch for 5 rounds, then bind off all stitches.

HAT BAND

Using color B, cast on 144 stitches, and work in garter stitch for 4 rows.

Work the Ska Diamond pattern chart. The chart will be repeated 12 times across.

Using color B, work in garter stitch for 3 rows, then bind off all stitches.

FINISHING

Using color A and a tapestry needle, sew the hem to the wrong side.

Weave in all the loose ends, being sure to weave at least 3" (7.5cm) of each end to ensure a tight hold during the felting process.

Felting

Please refer to the guidelines for *washing machine felting* on page 118.

Felt the hat and the band separately. Felting the pieces separately will allow you to have more control over the hatband size.

Shape by hand, especially pulling out any areas of that might have drawn in more tightly than desired during the felting process.

Shape the hat as shown in the photo: make a slight indentation on the crown, roll up the brim as desired, and pull on the brim periodically as the hat dries. Block the hatband lightly if needed.

If possible, allow the hat to air dry over a mannequin head, wig form, or kitchen bowl that measures about the same as the desired circumference of the hat—approximately 22" (56cm) for most adult heads.

When the pieces are dry, attach the hatband to the finished hat, pinning it in place. Sew it down using a sewing needle and thread.

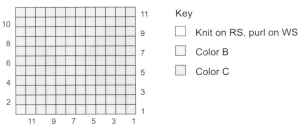

Key

☐ Knit on RS, purl on WS

☐ Color B

☐ Color C

shibori fez

The Shibori Fez represents one of my first true success

stories in the practice of shibori knitting

and has become a personal favorite.

I had previously written a similar slipped stitch pattern

in a silk pillow design and was eager to employ the

simple yet effective motif again.

The slipped stitch is assigned to the felting yarn in a

semi-solid color (of a medium to dark value), while the

little window shapes are knit in the

nonfelting fiber in a rich variegated handpaint (usually

of a lighter value). The fez is worked in the round.

The natural tendencies of the two varieties of fiber

synthesize beautifully in this piece—

form truly follows function! The woven slipped stitch

pattern is easy to memorize, and only one yarn is

worked at a time, making this a great take-along knit or

a perfect companion while watching a movie. Because

I have knit the fez many times, I can readily attest to

the versatility of working in practically any conceivable

combination of color—just make sure one color is

perceptibly darker than the other. If the fez sits a little

tall for your personal preference, just skip the last chart

repeat, and you'll get a subtler toque-style hat.

Level Intermediate

Knitted Measurements

Before felting

Circumference at the brim: 25½" (65cm)

Height: 9" (23cm)

Diameter at the crown: 7" (18cm)

After felting

Circumference at the brim: 22" (56cm)

Height: 6" (15cm)

Diameter at the crown: 6" (15cm)

Materials

Model on Left

Felting fiber

3 skeins of Alchemy Yarns Sanctuary, 70% merino, 30% silk, 1¾ oz (50g), 125 yds (114m), 09m Pewter (color A), **3** light

Nonfelting fiber

1 skein of Alchemy Yarns Silken Straw, 100% silk, 1¼ oz (40g), 236 yds (216m), 43c Waterlily (color B), **2** fine

This fiber is held double in this design. Please refer to the sidebar on page 27 for detailed instructions on easy winding of a double-stranded skein.

Model on Right

Felting fiber

3 skeins Alchemy Yarns Sanctuary, 70% merino, 30% silk, 1¾ oz (50g), 125 yds (114m), 12w Ocean Floor (color A), **3** light

Nonfelting fiber

1 skein Alchemy Yarns Pagoda, 100% silk boucle, 1¼ oz (40g), 183 yds (167m), 60c San Francisco Sky (color B), **4** medium

The fiber is NOT held double in this variation.

16" (40cm) circular needle in size US 6 (4mm) or size needed to obtain gauge

A set of double-pointed needles in size US 6 (4mm)

Stitch markers

Tapestry needle

Gauge

20 stitches and 34 rows = 4" (10cm) in garter stitch using nonfelting fiber.

Stitch Pattern

Woven Slip Stitch Pattern

(Worked over a multiple of 8 stitches in the round)

Note: Slip stitches *purlwise* with the yarn held in back.

Rounds 1–6 Using color B, *slip 2, k6; repeat from * to the end.

Rounds 7–10 Using color A, work 4 rounds in garter stitch (knit 1 round, purl 1 round).

Rounds 11–16 Using color B, k4, *slip 2, k6; repeat from * to the last 4 stitches, slip 2, k2.

Rounds 17–20 Work the same as rounds 7–10.

Repeat rounds 1–20 for woven slipstitch pattern.

HAT

Using color A, cast on 128 stitches. Place marker on the needle to indicate beginning of round. Join to work in the round by knitting the first stitch you cast on, being careful not to twist the cast-on edge.

Work in garter stitch for 20 rounds (knit 1 round, then purl 1 round.).

Work in Woven Slip Stitch pattern for 4 repeats (80 rounds).

Using color A, work 10 more rounds in garter stitch.

Bind off all stitches.

CROWN

Using color A and with the wrong side facing, pick up and knit 120 stitches evenly from the third garter ridge from the top. To do so, simply drop down from the very top of the hat to the third ridge formed, and pick up stitches from the top loops of this round on the inside of the hat. Place marker on the needle to indicate beginning of round.

Work 4 rounds in garter stitch.

Next 3 rounds

Rounds 1 and 2 Using color B, *slip 2, k18; repeat from * to the end.

Round 3 (set-up round) With color A, *knit 10, place marker on needle; repeat from * 10 times more, knit to end of the round.

Next 8 rounds

Round 1 *Knit to the last 2 stitches before the marker, k2tog; repeat from * to the end.

Round 2 Purl.

Repeat these 2 rounds 3 more times—72 stitches.

Slip all the stitches onto the double-pointed needles.

Next 11 rounds

Rounds 1 and 2 Change to color B, and work *slip 2, k16; repeat from * to the end.

Round 3 Change to color A, and knit.

Round 4 *Knit to the last 2 stitches before the marker, k2tog; repeat from * to the end.

Round 5 Purl.

Repeat the last 2 rounds 3 more times—24 stitches.

Remove markers, leaving only the marker at the beginning of the round.

Next 3 rounds

Round 1 Change to color B, and work *slip 2, k6; repeat from * to the end.

Round 2 Change to color A, and knit.

Round 3 K2tog 12 times—12 stitches.

Cut the yarn, and use a tapestry needle to thread the tail through the remaining 12 stitches. Pull tight to close the top of the hat.

FINISHING

Weave in all the loose ends, catching down at least 3" (7.5cm) of each end to ensure a tight hold during the felting process.

Felting

Please refer to the guidelines for *washing machine felting* on page 118.

If possible, allow the hat to air dry over a mannequin head, wig form, or kitchen bowl that measures about the same as the desired circumference of the hat—approximately 22" (56cm) for most adult heads.

"It is the pervading law of all things organic, and inorganic, of all things physical and metaphysical, of all things human and all things superhuman, of all true manifestations of the head, of the heart, of the soul, that the life is recognizable in its expression, that form ever follows function. This is the law."

—Louis Henry Sullivan, one of America's first modern architects

the poet's shawl

Every day for six weeks I knit this piece.

The daily practice was a discipline.

Some days I worked two rows, and some days I

worked more. The laceweight fiber was

like knitting a spider web—

it was an exercise in faith, knitting something

I could barely see, and had to simply trust and feel.

I would work and work, and sometimes it would

seem like I wasn't making much progress. I had to

let go of my attachment to how fast I could knit it.

Once finished, I spent a long time cultivating the

courage to felt the entire work.

To do so seemed like too much letting go. The

drape that is created from this combination of

fibers is so elegant, so ethereal; the risk that it

might transform too much made it difficult to

surrender to felting it. After months of living with

it not felted, I finally took the plunge, kissed it, and

tossed it in the washing machine. The felted result

is greatly satisfying and serves as manifestation

of letting go of attachment, in order to discover

something new and unexpected.

Level Intermediate

Knitted Measurements

Before felting

Back length: 24" (61cm)

Width from wing to wing: 88" (223.5cm)

Collar width: 14" (35.5cm)

Collar depth: 1¾" (4.5cm)

After felting

Back length: 25" (64 cm)

Width from wing to wing: 104" (165 cm)

Collar width: 22" (56 cm)

Collar depth: 2¼" (6 cm)

Materials

Felting fiber

3 skeins of Alchemy Yarns Haiku, 60% mohair, 40% silk, ⅞ oz (25g), 325 yds (297m), 42m silver (yarn A), ②fine

Nonfelting fiber

3 skeins of Alchemy Yarns Pagoda, 100% silk boucle, 1¼oz (40g), 183 yds (167m), 42m silver (yarn B), ④medium

24" (60cm) circular needle in size US 7 (4.5mm) or size needed to obtain gauge

A set of double-pointed needles in size US 5 (3.75mm)

Stitch markers

A hook-and-eye neck closure

Sewing needle and thread

Tapestry needle

Gauge

24 stitches and 32 rows = 4" (10cm) in stockinette stitch using yarn B and the circular needle

Notes

The mitered back is made first, then the "wings" are picked up and knit in a triangle form on either side. As a result, there are no seams to join.

Be careful to follow stranding instructions when using yarn A (yarn B is worked single stranded throughout).

When using more then 1 yarn in a row, make sure to twist yarns behind work to avoid holes.

SHAWL

Using 2 strands of yarn A held together and the circular needle, cast on 300 stitches.

Place 2 stitch markers on the needle, one on either side of the center 6 stitches.

Row 1 Knit to the last 2 stitches before the marker, ssk, slip marker (sl m), k6, sl m, k2tog, knit to the end.

Row 2 Knit.

Repeat these 2 rows twice more.

Change to yarn B, and repeat these 2 rows twice more.

Change to one strand of yarn A.

Contrasting panel rows

Row 1 Knit to the last 2 stitches before the marker, ssk, drop yarn A, sl m, join yarn B, k6, sl m, join a second ball of yarn A, k2tog, knit to the end.

Row 2 With yarn A, purl to the marker, sl m, using yarn B, k6, sl m, using yarn A, purl to the end.

Repeat these 2 rows until the piece measures 6" (15.25cm).

Change to yarn B.

V detail rows

Row 1 Knit to the last 2 stitches before the marker, ssk, sl m, k6, sl m, k2tog, knit to the end.

Row 2 Knit.

Repeat these 2 rows 4 more times.

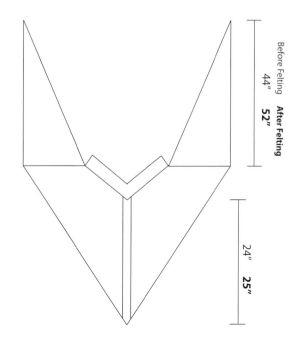

Work the contrasting panel rows again until the piece measures 13" (33cm), then work the V detail rows again.

Work the contrasting panel rows again until you have 154 stitches left, ending after a wrong side row.

Collar

Change to yarn B.

Next Row (Right Side) K2tog 37 times, remove marker, k6, remove marker, k2tog 37 times—80 stitches.

Work 19 rows in garter stitch, then bind off all stitches.

LEFT SIDE WING

Using yarn B, the circular needle and with the right side facing, pick up and knit 80 stitches along the left side edge.

Row 1 (Wrong Side) Knit.

Row 2 Ssk, knit to the end.

Repeat these 2 rows 4 more times.

Change to one strand of yarn A.

Next 2 rows:

Row 1 (Wrong Side) Purl.

Row 2 Ssk, knit to the end.

Repeat these 2 rows once more.

Repeat the last 14 rows until you have 10 stitches left.

Change to yarn B.

Next 2 rows

Row 1 (Wrong Side) Knit.

Row 2 Ssk, knit to the end.

Repeat these 2 rows until you have 3 stitches left.

Next row K3tog.

Fasten off.

Right Side Wing

Using yarn B, the circular needle and with the right side facing, pick up and knit 80 stitches along the right side edge.

Row 1 (Wrong Side) Knit.

Row 2 Knit across row until 2 sts remain, k2tog.

Repeat these 2 rows 4 more times.

Change to one strand of yarn A.

Next 2 rows

Row 1 (Wrong Side) Purl.

Row 2 Knit across row until 2 sts remain, k2tog.

Repeat these 2 rows once more.

Repeat the last 14 rows until you have 10 stitches left.

Change to yarn B.

Next 2 rows

Row 1 (Wrong Side) Knit.

Row 2 Knit across row until 2 sts remain, k2tog.

Repeat these 2 rows until you have 3 stitches left.

Next row K3tog.

Fasten off.

I-CORD PIPING

Using 1 strand of yarn A and 1 strand of yarn B held together, and a double-pointed needle, cast on 3 stitches. Work an I-cord (see glossary, page 121) 30" (76.25cm) long, or until the cord is long enough to have a relaxed fit under the collar's edge. Bind off all stitches.

FINISHING

Weave in all the loose ends.

Piping embellishment

With right side facing, position the I-cord piping just below collar edge. Pin it, adjusting placement as necessary. Sew it lightly in place using a sewing needle and thread. Overlap the excess piping, if necessary, to the inside of the shawl.

Felting

Please refer to the guidelines for *washing machine felting* on page 118. Allow to dry completely.

Attach the hook and eye at the ends of the piping.

If you drop stitches as you knit, go back and catch them. Working with such a fine fiber, it is easy to do. I catch mine as I notice them, and hold them with a stitch marker (I prefer the round ones, that spiral for closure.) When I finish knitting, I work the stitch back into the fabric with a tapestry needle and matching thread, weaving in the ends so that the dropped stitch is undetectable (see appendix, page 118).

Take shibori to the next level—make the Portrait Scarf (page 110), the S'il Vous Plait Kimono (page 103), or the Fortune Cookie Scarf (page 112).

subtle *shibori*

Double Dog Dare You Capelet **84**

I Wanna Hold Your Hand Warmers **88**

Contemplative Wrap **92**

Wild Side Skirt **98**

S'il Vous Plait Kimono **103**

Portrait Scarf **110**

Fortune Cookie Scarf **112**

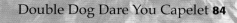

adventures in color, composition, and construction

subtle *shibori*

adventures in color, composition, and construction

Shibori knitting has no limits when the door is opened wide to a myriad of shaping opportunities and color bravado. While continuing to celebrate the blending of fiber and color, this chapter explores what happens when you change directions. By literally turning the knitting on its side, you start to play with the weaving concepts of warp and weft—the two components of a woven piece that work in perpendicular directions. With knitting, this change of knit direction interfaces with a yarn's tendency to move in particular directions when it is felted. The end results are sublime—ruffles, ripples, and spiraling shapes magically appear when the knit is felted. This exciting direction-al effect is most evident in the Portrait Scarf (page 110), but is explored subtly in the Wild Side Skirt (page 98), the Contempla-tive Wrap (page 92), and the hand warmers (page 88), to name a few projects.

Changing knit direction is made even more fascinating when we incorporate the methods explored in the first two chapters, as well as venture into more complex color opportunities. My friend, the great designer Kaffe Fassett, has long inspired me reinterpret knitting, design, and color. I've always felt con-nected to his other life as a painter, as I once made my living as a sculptor. Kaffe's ability to knit a sophisticated palette with skill and confidence is a great complement to the way he writes his knitting patterns. Most of the time, he dutifully details every color used in a piece. But every now and then he just puts forth his own creative expression, and gives the reader only a general idea of how to approach color. Rather than spell out all 47 hues in a design, he encourages the reader to find her or his personal aesthetic, offering general suggestions, such as grouping fiber into three categories: light, medium, and dark. Thus, the knitter is able to take on more creative responsibility and make some-thing unique and original while being held in the wisdom and experience of Kaffe's personal exploration.

The offerings in this chapter will hopefully inspire knitters to explore personal color aesthetic in a similar way. For instance, I love green. It's been my favorite color all my life, unabashed and uncontested. I work in it every chance I get. But if your favorite color is blue, then work in blue! Take what I have done with my love of green, and draw inspiration from the pictured work while bringing together harmonious colors that will cel-ebrate your love of blue.

Metaphorically, this final chapter is about celebrating personal sincerity and truth in one's exploration. If you gravitate toward a different palette, bow to your preference and be truthful to your own creativity. The knitwear pieces collected will serve you faithfully, as you find your way a little further down the shibori path.

The Wild Side Skirt (page 98) is a classic example of turning knitting on its side.

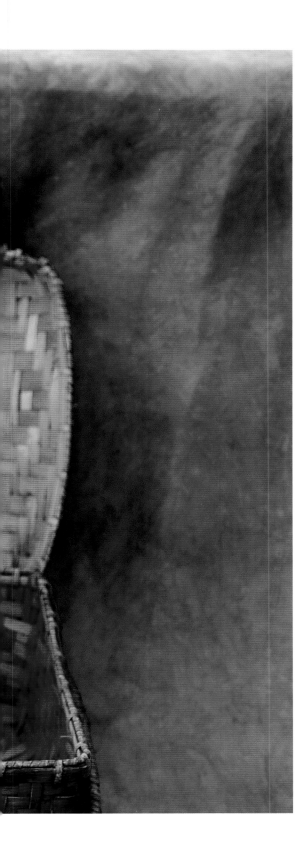

double dog dare you capelet

In the summer of 2006, I spent some time in Barcelona and

found a home away from home in that vibrant city.

I rented a flat by the beach, and just around the corner,

there was a cool coffee house. Every morning,

I sat at an outdoor table with a double espresso

and knit this capelet for my tiny dog at home in California,

whom I missed terribly.

I had just made the Portrait Scarf (page 110)

before we left on our trip to Spain and was very excited

about the shibori ruffle in that piece.

So I took the same concept—a simple rectangle in a felting

fiber—and made it long enough

to fit my pup's neck. Afterward, with a nonfelting silk, I

picked up and knit a ruffle slightly more flared than the one

in the Portrait Scarf. When I finished the first ruffle, I didn't

want to break my ritual of knitting at the coffee house in the

mornings—so I added another ruffle! After all, Barcelona is

one of those cities that abides by the saying:

"If it's worth doing, it's worth overdoing."

This piece is also great as a knit bracelet. Simply make the

smallest size for a dazzling ruffled cufflet!

Level Intermediate

Knitted Measurements

Measurements are given for XS (S, M, L, XL) sizes in that order

Before felting

Neck circumference: 11 (14, 17, 21, 24)" (28 [35.5, 43, 53.5, 61]cm)

After felting

To fit dog's neck circumference: 6–9 (10–12, 13–15, 16–18, 19–21)" (15–23 [25.5–30.5, 33–38, 40.5–45.5, 48.5–53.5]cm)

Materials

Felting fiber

1 skein of Alchemy Yarns Sanctuary, 70% merino, 30% silk, 1¾ oz (50g), 125 yds (114m), 36f Lantern (color A), (3) light

Nonfelting fiber

1 (1, 1, 2, 2) skeins of Alchemy Yarns Silken Straw, 100% silk, 1¼ oz (35.5g), 236 yds (216m), 11m Full Metal Alchemist (color B), (2) fine

Knitting needles in size US 4 (3.5mm) or size needed to obtain gauge

1 small button, ⅜" (10mm) in diameter—shown is a Moving Mud design in hand-blown glass

Tapestry needle

1 shoelace (to hold the buttonhole open during felting)

Gauge

24 stitches and 32 rows = 4" (10cm) in stockinette stitch using color A before felting

Notes

When selecting a size, please use the post-felting neck measurements.

Both ruffles are made on the same side of the collar.

When ruffles are knit, increases are made on only one end of the rectangle. Please see The Portrait Scarf (page 110) for an explanation for this shaping.

COLLAR

Using color A, cast on 12 stitches and work even in stockinette stitch for 10 (13, 17, 21, 24)" (25.5 [33, 43, 53.5, 61]cm).

Create buttonholes

Next row (Right Side) K2, bind off 2 stitches, k4, bind off 2 stitches, k2.

Next row P2, cast on 2 stitches, p4, cast on 2 stitches, p2.

Work 6 rows even in stockinette stitch, then bind off all stitches.

Fold the collar in half lengthwise, putting the wrong sides together and lining up the buttonholes.

Use a tapestry needle to sew the long side of the collar band closed. Sew the two layers together around the buttonholes with a whip stitch.

RUFFLE I

Using color B and with the right side facing, pick up and knit 88 (112, 144, 176, 200) stitches along one edge of the collar.

Row 1 (Wrong Side) Knit.

Row 2 Knit to the last 2 stitches, kfb, k1.

Repeat these 2 rows 11 (14, 17, 20, 23) more times, then bind off all stitches.

RUFFLE II

Using color B and with the right side facing, pick up and knit 88 (112, 144, 176, 200) stitches just underneath the picked up row for Ruffle I.

Row 1 (Wrong Side) Knit.

Row 2 Knit to the last 2 stitches, kfb, k1.

Repeat these 2 rows 14 (17, 20, 22, 26) more times, then bind off all stitches.

FINISHING

Use a tapestry needle to weave in all the loose ends, being sure to weave at least 3" (7.5cm) of each end to ensure a tight hold during the felting process. Thread the shoelace through the buttonhole, to prevent it from closing during the felting process. Secure the shoelace tightly.

Felting

Please refer to the guidelines for *washing machine felting* on page 118.

When the capelet is dry, try it on the dog. You may fold back the end of the felted edge, if desired, for a more custom fit and sew it in place. Pin the button in place and check again for a proper fit. Sew on the button.

Side Accent for Version I Only

Work 1 row in single crochet along the seam of the three-needle bind-off, then fasten off.

FINISHING

Use a tapestry needle to weave in all the loose ends, being sure to weave at least 3" (7.5cm) of each end to ensure a tight hold during the felting process.

Felting

Please refer to the guidelines for *washing machine felting* on page 118.

Felting will require a bit of patience, and the time will vary depending on your machine. Please allow two 5-minute gentle cycles for felting, checking frequently during the second cycle. Stop when your handwarmers are the desired size. Do not overfelt! Allow the hand warmers to air dry, trying them on while they are slightly damp to ensure a perfect fit.

Distinguishing different fiber types

Not sure what fiber you have? Here's a tip on how to distinguish silk protein from wool protein. Try a simple burn test. If it smells like burning hair, it's wool. Silk will smell much funkier and not quite as organic as the wool. Both silk and wool will leave a powdery ash when burned, and will extinguish on their own when the flame is removed. A synthetic fiber will need to be extinguished.

Ever more delightful possibilities in shaping are offered in this wrap, which doubles beautifully as a lap blanket. Building on the basic shibori ruffle concept, this unique piece is a bold foray into working with multiple colors. The design rests in the comfortable realm of simple knit construction, with stockinette stitch and garter stitch being the primary tools. A lacy crochet border is incorporated, encouraging the knitter to open to the thought of felting lace—a radical concept!

When I was knitting this piece, I found it enticing to work with a bright yet comforting palette. When choosing yarn for the piece, pick colors that reflect the mood you desire—calm, cool, and harmonious; quiet, subtle, and serene; or vibrant, intense, and saturated. Regardless of the palette, the rhythm and soft unfolding of the knit is a grounding and pleasant experience.

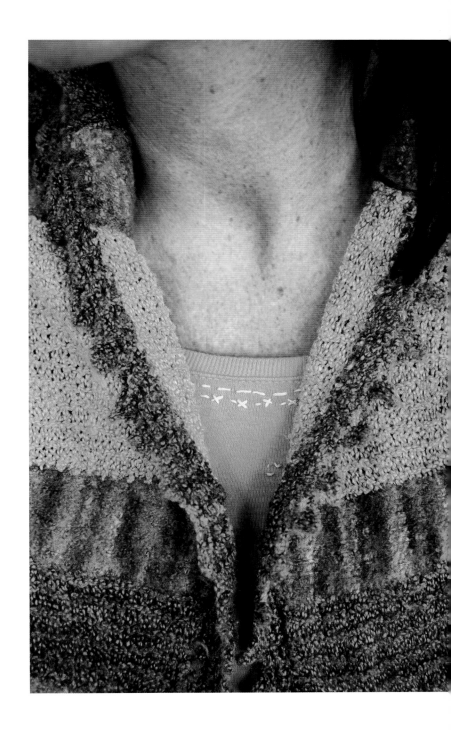

Level Intermediate

Knitted Measurements

Before felting

32" x 36" (81cm x 91cm)

After felting

34" (86cm) at widest point and 21" (53.5cm) at narrowest point x 48" (122cm)

Materials

Felting fiber

3 skeins Alchemy Yarns Sanctuary, 70% merino, 30% silk, 1¾ oz (50g), 125 yds (114m), 10c Costa Brava (color A), **⟨3⟩** light

Nonfelting fiber

3 skeins Alchemy Yarns Pagoda, 100% silk boucle, 1¼ oz (40g), 183 yds (167m), 30w Spruce (color B), **⟨4⟩** medium

2 skeins each of Alchemy Yarns Pagoda, 100% silk boucle, 1¼ oz (40g), 183 yds (167m), 28w Teal Tide (color C) and 50e Sour Grass (color D), **⟨4⟩** medium

1 skein of Alchemy Yarns Pagoda, 100% silk boucle, 1¼ oz (40g), 183 yds (167m), 19w Soft Turquoise (color E), **⟨4⟩** medium

32" (80cm) circular needle in size US 6 (4mm) or size needed to obtain gauge

A set of double-pointed needles in the same size (for ease in constructing the thin strips)

Crochet hook in size F-5 (3.75mm)

Tapestry needle

Gauge

20 stitches and 34 rows = 4" (10cm) in garter stitch using color A before felting

Notes

Contrary to popular felting belief, this piece will actually grow rather than shrink after felting. Please refer to page 119 for detailed information about expectations and shrinkage in shibori felting.

The piece is constructed in a series of panels, some of which are knit in narrow stockinette stitch strips. Other panels are knit in a perpendicular direction, picked up and knit alongside the long edges of the strips. All panels are joined together before felting. Because the shrinking (felting)

fiber travels in one direction, the nonfelting fiber responds to the pull of the felting fiber, forming the ruffled effect.

When working the stripes in sections 1 and 17, carry color E up the side of the piece. All other colors should be joined as needed, with ends woven in for each stripe.

Please look at the color chart as you knit. Although the written directions will not always move in numerical sequence, you will soon catch on to the predictable rhythm of the construction that is necessary for the shibori effect.

WRAP

Section 2

(Section 2 is made before section 1, due to the necessary shibori technique)

Using color A and a double-pointed needle, cast on 4 stitches, and work in stockinette stitch for 32" (81cm).

Bind off all stitches

Section 1

Using color E and the circular needle and with the right side facing, pick up and knit 190 stitches along one of the long sides of section 2.

Work in garter stitch, using the following color sequence:

Using color E, knit 7 rows.

Change to color D, and knit 2 rows.

Change to color E, and knit 2 rows.

Change to color C, and knit 2 rows.

Change to color E, and knit 2 rows.

Change to color B, and knit 4 rows.

Change to color E, and knit 10 rows.

Change to color B, and knit 4 rows.

Change to color E, and knit 2 rows.

Change to color C, and knit 2 rows.

Change to color E, and knit 2 rows.

Change to color D, and knit 2 rows.

Change to color E, and knit 7 rows.

Bind off all stitches.

Section 3

Using color C and the circular needle, and with the right side facing, pick up and knit 190 stitches along opposite side of the long rectangle of section 1.

Work in garter stitch for 11 rows, then bind off all stitches.

Section 4

Using color A and the double-pointed needles, cast on 10 stitches, and work in stockinette stitch for 32" (81cm).

Bind off all stitches

Using mattress stitch on the wrong side, sew the bound off edge of section 3 to one long edge of section 4.

Section 5

Using color D, and with the right side facing, pick up and knit 190 stitches along the free long edge of section 4.

Work 27 rows in garter stitch, then bind off all stitches.

Section 6

Work the same as section 4, then sew together sections 5 and 6.

Section 7

Using color C, work the same as for section 5, working 15 rows in garter stitch.

Bind off all stitches.

Section 8

Work the same as section 4, then sew sections 7 and 8 together.

Section 9

Using color B, work the same as for section 5, working 23 rows in garter stitch.

| Section 1 |
| Section 2 |
| Section 3 |
| Section 4 |
| Section 5 |
| Section 6 |
| Section 7 |
| Section 8 |
| Section 9 |
| Section 10 |
| Section 11 |
| Section 12 |
| Section 13 |
| Section 14 |
| Section 15 |
| Section 16 |
| Section 17 |

After felting: 48"
Before felting: 36"

32"   **21 - 34"**

Key
- ☐ Color A
- ▨ Color B
- ☐ Color C
- ☐ Color D
- ☐ Color E

Bind off all stitches.

Section 10

Work the same as section 4, then sew sections 9 and 10 together.

Section 11

Work the same as section 7.

Section 12

Work the same as section 4, then sew sections 11 and 12 together.

Section 13

Work the same as section 5.

Section 14

Work the same as section 4, then sew sections 13 and 14 together.

Section 15

Work the same as section 3.

Section 16

Work the same as section 2 then sew sections 15 and 16 together.

Section 17

Work the same as section 1.

CROCHET PICOT EDGING

Using color B and with the right side facing, work 3 rounds in single crochet around the entire piece. Work 3 single crochets into each corner for the turns.

Next round *Sc into each of the next 2 stitches, ch 3, sl st into the top of the last sc; repeat from * around.

Fasten off.

FINISHING

Use a tapestry needle to weave in all the loose ends, catching down at least 3" (7.5cm) of each end to ensure a tight hold during the felting process.

Felting

Please refer to the guidelines for *washing machine felting* on page 118.

Shape by hand, especially pulling out any areas that might have drawn in more tightly than desired during the felting process.

Allow the wrap to air dry gently and slowly. Block lightly to size, if needed. The silk fiber responds beautifully to an iron and softens tremendously when ironed on a cool setting.

I always find it helpful to make a little color key before beginning a piece with multiple colors or yarns. Simply tape a short piece of each fiber to an index card and label each piece with its color name and its color identification letter (for example, color B). The color key card can be used not only to keep track of the colors, but also as a helpful bookmark.

wild side skirt

Edgy urban meets wabi-sabi aesthetic in this compelling lace mesh skirt. No shrinking violet here, this piece is meant to seriously shift your thoughts about shibori—literally, as the design actually does shift dramatically in terms of construction.

I adore the quality of fabric rendered by the shibori method, especially in this garment—the contrast of mesh silk with fused felted fiber is gorgeous. The sensuous drape and flow of the panels allows for a very fresh perspective on what constitutes a felted garment, as the fabric created is delicate and truly ethereal, with incredible movement.

Using the classic shibori method of changing direction to create a ruffle, the panels are joined in a circle and fitted to a waistband that's embellished with a whimsical I-cord. A little sewing experience is helpful when making this piece.

Level Experienced

Knitted Measurements

Measurements are given for XS (S, M, L) sizes in that order

Before felting

Waist: 28 (32, 36, 40)" (71 [81, 91, 101.5]cm)

Length: 16 (16, 17, 17)" (40.5 [40.5, 43, 43]cm)

Panel width: 4" (10cm)

After felting

Waist: 36 (40, 44, 48)" (91 [101.5, 112, 122]cm)

Length: 12 (12, 13, 13)" (30.5 [30.5, 33, 33]cm)

Panel width: 5" (12.5cm)

Materials

Felting fiber

1 (1, 2, 2) skeins of Alchemy Yarns Sanctuary, 70% merino, 30% silk, 1¾ oz (50g), 125 yds (114m), 65e Dragon (color A), 【3】 light

Nonfelting fiber

3 (4, 5, 6) skeins of Yarns Silken Straw, 100% silk, 1¼ oz (40g), 236 yds (216m), 76e Citrine (color B), 【2】 fine

24" (60cm) circular needle in size US 6 (4mm) or size needed to obtain gauge

A set of double-pointed needles in the same size

¾" (2cm) wide elastic band in a length that is 2" (5cm) longer than desired waist measurement

T-pins

Sewing needle and thread

Tapestry needle

Gauge

24 stitches and 28 rows = 4" (10cm) in stockinette stitch using color A before felting

Notes

The skirt will grow in width after it is felted. When selecting a size, please choose it using the post-felting measurements. Measure your natural waist or part of your body where you want the skirt to rest. The elasticized waistband will ensure a custom fit.

The skirt is made up of several panels. Each panel starts with a narrow stockinette stitch strip worked in the felting fiber. Then the nonfelting fiber is picked up and knit along one long edge of the stockinette strip to complete the panel. The panels are then sewn together to form a tube. This type of construction encourages a wonderful shibori ruffle in the nonfelting fiber, and plays on the natural tendencies of the two fibers used in the piece.

The use of double-pointed needles makes knitting more efficient when constructing the narrow panels of felting fiber.

Weaving in the ends as you work will save a great deal of time when the piece is completed.

Stitch Patterns

Diagonal Mesh Lace Pattern

(Worked over an even number of stitches)

Row 1 K1, *yo, k2tog; repeat from * to the last stitch, k1.

Row 2 Purl.

Row 3 K1, *k2tog, yo; repeat from * to the last stitch, k1.

Row 4 Purl.

Repeat rows 1–4 for diagonal lace mesh pattern.

PANELS—MAKE 7 (8, 9, 10)

Using color A and a double-pointed needle, cast on 5 stitches.

Work in stockinette stitch for 16 (16, 17, 17)" (40.5 [40.5, 43, 43]cm).

Bind off all stitches.

Using color B and the circular needle, and with the right side facing, pick up and knit 92 stitches (approximately 5 stitches for every 6 rows) along one long side edge of the stockinette stitch strip.

Purl one row.

Work 24 rows in diagonal mesh lace pattern, then bind off all stitches.

I-CORD FOR SPIRAL ROSE EMBELLISHMENT

Using color A and a double-pointed needle, cast on 3 stitches. Work an I-cord (see glossary, page 121) 44 (48, 52, 56)" (112 [122, 132, 142]cm) long, then bind off all stitches.

GARTER STITCH WAISTBAND

Using color A and a double-pointed needle, cast on 14 stitches, and work in garter stitch for 28 (32, 36, 40)" (71 [81, 91.5, 101.5]cm).

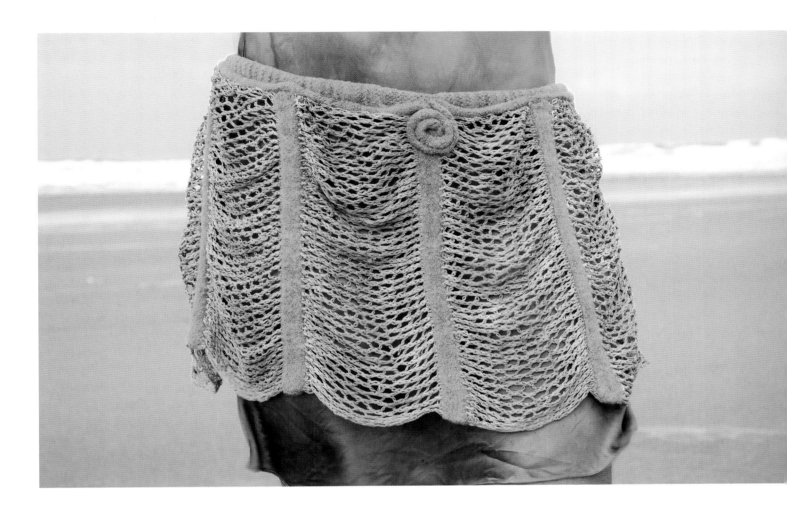

Important note: The waistband will stretch slightly in length after felting and can be adjusted when it is joined to the skirt.

Bind off all stitches.

FINISHING

Using a tapestry needle and yarn A, sew the panels together into a tube, sewing approximately 5 color B stitches to every 6 color A rows.

Do not attach the I-cord or the waistband to the skirt at this point.

Use a tapestry needle to weave in all the loose ends, being sure to weave at least 3" (7.5cm) of each end to ensure a tight hold during the felting process.

28 (32, 36, 40)" **36 (40, 44, 48)"**

Before felting: 16 (16, 17, 17)"
After felting: 12 (12, 13, 13)"

7 (8, 9, 10) panels

Key

☐ Color A

☐ Color B

Felting

Please refer to the guidelines for *washing machine felting* on page 118.

Allow all the pieces to air dry separately and completely before assembling.

Spiral Rose Embellishment

Decide where the center front of the skirt will be, and mark it with a T-pin.

Pin one end of the I-cord at the center, then pin the I-cord around the top edge of the skirt, ending at the center again. This will not use up the entire I-cord. Twist the remaining end of the I-cord on itself to create a spiral (see photo.) With a sewing needle and matching thread, sew the I-cord spiral in place, catching it from various sides, to ensure hold. Cut the I-cord if it is too long.

Waistband Assembly

Cut the elastic to the natural waist measurement, plus 2" (5cm).

Fold the waistband in half, insert the elastic in the middle, and pin it shut.

Try on the waistband for a proper fit, adjusting the elastic as necessary. Remember that the ends of the elastic need to overlap by at least 1" (2.5cm) when sewing them together.

Remove the elastic from inside the waistband. Sew the long edges of the folded waistband together to make a casing, leaving a 1" (2.5cm) opening to insert the elastic later.

Pin the waistband to the skirt, adjusting the skirt to swag as desired. This swag is meant to be decorative as well as functional, and gives you a bit more opportunity to customize your fit. I allowed the mesh panels to hang down and sewed them to the bottom edge of the waistband, while sewing the felted strips to the top edge of the waistband. Doing this exaggerated the undulating hemline of the skirt.

When you are happy with the look, carefully try on the skirt again, and adjust it for fit.

If the garter waistband is too long, cut it with scissors, being careful to reposition the pinned mesh panels. Adjust the elastic as needed, and sew the ends of the waistband together.

Once you are happy with the fit, sew the waistband by hand to the skirt using a sewing needle and thread. Insert the elastic into the casing and sew the ends together, being sure to overlap at least 1" (2.5cm) of the elastic for a secure hold. If possible, use a sewing machine to sew the elastic because it will provide a more secure hold.

Using a sewing needle and thread, sew the casing opening shut.

On the door of my studio, I have a tiny card that reads: "What are the sections sections of? Imagine a caterpillar moving." I love this saying and think about it almost every time I open my studio door. It is a call to understand the majesty of interconnectedness. Everything is relative to something else. I thought of this principle when making this particular design, the Wild Side Skirt. By alternating panels of differing materials, the effects of the two kinds of fiber employed gave a visual example to the question, "What are the sections sections of?"

s'il vous plait kimono

In many ways, Shibori is the knitting equivalent of not

knowing. Fortunately, there are many characteristics

we can know about this creative art form—

formulas to follow and ways to be guided to success.

However, when it comes to shaped and fitted

garments—particularly regarding sizing—

shibori becomes a slippery slope. Making a one-size-

fits-all shawl is one thing; dropping a bundle of money

or depleting one's cherished stash on

an unpredictable cardigan is another.

In this design, I have minimized the risk involved by

limiting the shibori aspect to one pivotal

and dramatic detail: the obi.

The kimono itself is knit from a combination of felting

and nonfelting fibers, but it is not felted.

This combination of silk and mohair fibers is luxurious

and texturally pleasing, worked on a large needle, and

gives the piece a splendid drape and hand.

What makes the piece shibori is the obi. A glorious

and unexpected palette of felting fibers are worked

together in a dynamic slip stitch pattern, resulting in

a sophisticated and beautiful obi, with resist method

flowers worked at the tie.

Level Experienced

Knitted Measurements

Measurements are given for S (M, L) in that order

Chest: 36 (41, 46)" (91 [104, 117]cm)

Length: 30 (31, 32)" (76 [79, 81]cm)

Sleeve length: 14½ (15, 15½)" (37 [38, 39.5]cm) from the armhole

Obi Before felting

7½" × 24 (28, 32)" (19cm × 61 [71, 81]cm)

Obi After felting

3½" × 28 (32, 36)" (71cm × 71 [81, 91]cm)

Materials

Kimono

5 (6, 7) skeins of Alchemy Yarns Silk Purse, 100% silk, 1¾ oz (50g), 138 yds (126m), 100c Azalea Trail (color A), (3) light

2 (3, 3) skeins of Alchemy Yarns Haiku, 60% mohair, 40% silk, ⅞ oz (25g), 325 yds (297m), 51c A Breath of Fire (color B), (2) fine

Obi

1 skein each of Alchemy Yarns Sanctuary, 70% merino, 30% silk, 1¾ oz (50g), 125 yds (114m), 25a Delphinium (color C), 88a Hush (color D), 28w Teal Tide (color E), 76e Citrine (color F) and 38a Foxglove (color G), (3) light

16" (40cm) and 24" (60cm) circular needle in size US 10 (6mm) or size needed to obtain gauge

16" (40cm) and 32" (80cm) circular needle in size US 6 (4mm) or size needed to obtain gauge

Approximately 20 small marbles (approximately ⅜" [1cm] in diameter)

Approximately 20 small rubber bands

Waste yarn (must not be a felting fiber)

6 standard hook-and-eye closures

Sewing needle and thread to match color C (or dominant color in obi)

Tapestry needle

Gauge

Kimono

16 stitches and 20 rows = 4" (10cm) in stockinette stitch using one strand of color A and color B held together, with the larger needles

Obi

22 stitches and 28 rows = 4" (10cm) in woven slip stitch pattern (page 107) using the smaller needle before felting

Notes

Do not felt the kimono. Felt only the obi.

The kimono is knit from the top down, eliminating the need for setting in and sewing the sleeves.

Use waste yarn in place of stitch holders for this garment to allow the work in progress to lay flat.

KIMONO

Yoke

Using one strand of color A and one strand of color B held together, and the larger 24" (60cm) circular needle, cast on 44 (48, 50) stitches.

Set-up row (Wrong Side) P3, pm, p 8 (9, 9), pm, p 22 (24, 26), pm, p 8 (9, 9), pm, p3.

Row 1 *Knit to the last stitch before the marker, m1, k1, sl marker, k 1, m1; repeat from * 3 more times, knit to the end.

Row 2 Purl.

Repeat these 2 rows twice more.

Next 8 rows

Row 1 (Right Side) K1, m1, *knit to the last stitch before the marker, m1, k1, sl marker, k 1, m1; repeat from * 3 more times, knit to the last stitch, m1, k1.

Row 2 and all WS rows Purl.

Rows 3, 5, and 7 *Knit to the last stitch before the marker, m1, k1, sl marker, k1, m1; repeat from * 3 more times, knit to the end.

Repeat these 8 rows until you have 64 (68, 72) stitches for the back center section, 50 (53, 55) for each sleeve section, and 30 (31, 32) for each front section.

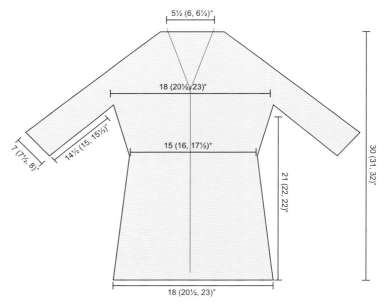

Row 1 (Right Side) K to marker, remove marker, use a darning needle to place 50 (53, 55) sleeve stitches on waste yarn, remove marker, cast on 4 (5, 6) stitches, pm, cast on 4 (5, 6) stitches, k64 (68, 72) back stitches, remove marker, place 50 (53, 55) sleeve stitches on waste yarn, remove marker, cast on 4 (5, 6) stitches, pm, cast on 4 (5, 6) stitches, k30 (31, 32)—140 (150, 160) stitches.

Lower Body

Next 8 rows

Row 1 (Right Side) K1, m1, knit to last stitch, m1, k1.

Row 2 Purl.

Rows 3–8 Work in stockinette stitch.

Repeat these 8 rows 1 (2, 3) more times—144 (156, 168) stitches.

Next 4 rows

Row 1 (Right Side) *Knit to the last 3 stitches before the marker, ssk, k1, sl marker, k1, k2tog; repeat from * once more, knit to the end.

Rows 2–4 Work in stockinette stitch.

Repeat these 4 rows 5 (6, 6) more times—120 (128, 140) stitches.

Work even in stockinette stitch until the lower body measures 8 (8½, 8½)" (20.5 [21.5, 21.5]cm) from the armhole cast-on edge.

Next 4 rows

Row 1 (Right Side) *Knit to the last stitch before the marker, m1, k1, sl marker, k1, m1; repeat from * once more, knit to the end.

Rows 2–4 Work in stockinette stitch.

Repeat these 4 rows 5 (6, 6) more times—144 (156, 168) stitches.

Work even in stockinette stitch until the lower body measures 20 (21, 21)" (51 [53.5, 53.5]cm]) from the armhole cast-on edge, or to desired length, ending on a wrong-side row.

Bind off all stitches.

SLEEVES (MAKE 2)

Place the stitches for one sleeve onto the larger 16" (40cm) needles.

Pick up 4 (5, 6) stitches from the armhole cast-on edge, pm, pick up 4 (5, 6) stitches from the armhole cast-on edge, knit the 50 (53, 55) sleeve stitches with the right side facing—58 (63, 67) stitches.

Join to work in the round by knitting the first stitch you cast on, and place another marker. (This marker should be in a different color or design to denote the beginning of the round.)

Next 6 rounds

Rounds 1–5 Knit.

Round 6 Knit to the last 3 stitches before the marker at the center of underarm, ssk, k1, sl marker, k1, k2tog, knit to the end.

Repeat these 6 rounds 4 (5, 6) more times—48 (51, 53) stitches.

Work even in stockinette stitch (knitting every round) until the sleeve measures 13½ (14, 14½)" (34.5 [35.5, 37]cm) from the armhole.

Bind off all stitches.

HEMS

Bottom Edge of Kimono

Using color A *only* and the smaller 32" (80cm) needles and with the right side facing, pick up and knit 144 (156, 168) stitches across the bound-off lower edge.

Work 6 rows in stockinette stitch.

Next row (Wrong Side) Knit to form the turning ridge.

Work 5 rows in stockinette stitch, then bind off all stitches.

Neck and Collar Edge

Using color A and the smaller 32" (80cm) needles and with the right side facing, pick up and knit 130 (136, 142) stitches up the right front edge, 44 (48, 50) stitches across the cast-on edge, and 130 (136, 142) stitches down the left front edge.

Work 6 rows in stockinette stitch.

Next row (Wrong Side) Knit to form the turning ridge.

Work 5 rows in stockinette stitch, then bind off all stitches.

Sleeve Edge

Using color A and the smaller 16" (40cm) needles and with the right side facing, pick up and knit 48 (51, 53) stitches around the sleeve edge.

Join to work in the round by knitting the first stitch you picked up, and place a marker on the needle to denote the beginning of the round.

Work 6 rounds in stockinette stitch.

Next round Purl to form the turning ridge.

Work 5 rounds in stockinette stitch, then bind off all stitches.

KIMONO FINISHING

Sew the hems to the wrong side.

Sew shut the openings at the underarms.

Weave in all the loose ends.

Kimono closure

Use a sewing needle and thread to sew 4 hook-and-eye closures onto the kimono, beginning at the bottom of the V-neck, then spacing them approximately 3" (7.5cm) apart down the length of the kimono, or as desired.

OBI

Woven Slip Stitch Pattern (worked over a multiple of 6 stitches +2)

Section A

Rows 1 and 3 Using color F, *slip 2 wyib, k4; repeat from * to end of row, ending slip 2.

Rows 2 and 4 Using color F, *slip 2 wyif, p4; repeat from * to end of row, ending slip 2.

Section B

Rows 1 and 3 Using color D, k2, *k1, slip 2 wyib, k3; repeat from * to end of row.

Rows 2 and 4 Using color D, p2, *p1, slip 2 wyif, p3; repeat from * to end of row.

Obi

Using color E and the size 6 (4 mm) 16" needles, cast on 176 (206, 236) stitches and work 4 rows in stockinette stitch.

Join color F, leaving color E not in use on the right-hand edge of work, and work Section A of Woven Slip Stitch Pattern.

With color E, work 4 rows in stockinette stitch.

Work 2 rows in garter stitch using color B.

Change to color C and work in stockinette stitch for 4 rows.

Join color D, leaving color C not in use on the right-hand edge of work, and work Section B of Woven Slip Stitch Pattern.

With color C, work 4 rows in stockinette stitch.

Work 2 rows in garter stitch using color B.

With color E, work 4 rows in stockinette stitch.

Join color F, leaving color E not in use on the right-hand edge of work, and work Section A of Woven Slip Stitch Pattern.

With color E, work 4 rows in stockinette stitch.

Bind off all stitches.

Obi Ties

Determine which edge is to be the top of the obi (either side is fine, but you need to establish this orientation, so that your flowers and leaves will be appropriately matched when the obi is tied).

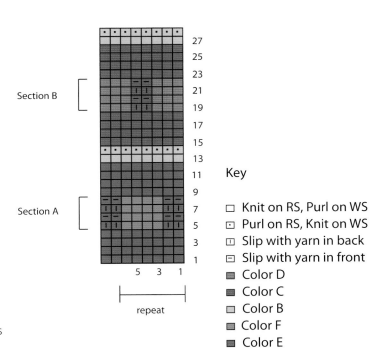

Key

☐ Knit on RS, Purl on WS
⊡ Purl on RS, Knit on WS
⊡ Slip with yarn in back
⊟ Slip with yarn in front
◼ Color D
◼ Color C
◻ Color B
◼ Color F
◼ Color E

Flower One

With color B and smallest needles, pick up 4 stitches at the right end of the obi, at the garter ridge of the same color/fiber. Work in I-cord for 8½" (22cm). Cut color B.

To make a flower, with color F and size 6 (4mm) needle, work back and forth in stockinette stitch over the 4 stitches from the I-cord for 4 rows. Increase 1 stitch at each end (kfb) every right-side row until there are 14 stitches. Change to color C and increase 1 stitch at each end (kfb) every right-side row until there are 18 stitches. Work even without shaping in stockinette stitch for 2 rows.

Next row (Increase Row) Kfb in each stitch—36 stitches.

Work in stockinette stitch until color C measures 2" (5cm). Bind off all stitches.

To make stamen and pistil of flower, with color E and size 6 (4mm) needle, pick up 3 stitches inside the flower, beginning ½" (1.5cm) above the place where you joined color C. Work these 3 stitches in I-cord for 2" (5cm). Change to color D and work in stockinette stitch for 4 rows. Increase 1 stitch (kfb) at each end of every right-side row until there are 9 stitches. Work even in stockinette stitch without shaping for 2 rows.

Decrease 1 stitch (k2tog) at each end of every right side row until there are 3 stitches. Bind off all stitches leaving a 6" (15cm) tail. Thread the tail through a tapestry needle and tack the point to the first row of color D.

Flower Two

Repeat as for flower one, on the left end of the top of the obi.

Leaves One

With color B and smallest needles, pick up 4 stitches at right end of the obi (lower edge), at the garter ridge of the same color/fiber. Work in I-cord for 8" (20cm). Cut color B.

To make the first leaf, with color E and size 6 (4 mm) needle, work in stockinette stitch over 4 stitches from I-cord for 4 rows. Increase 1 stitch at the left edge only of every right-side row twice—6 stitches. Increase 1 stitch (kfb) at both edges of the next right-side row—8 stitches. Work 3 rows in stockinette stitch without shaping.

Next row K2tog, k6.

Purl the next row.

Repeat these 2 rows until there are 2 stitches remaining. K2tog, and fasten off.

To make the second leaf, repeat as for the first leaf.

If a third leaf is desired (as shown on one side of the obi), with color E and size 6 needle, pick up and knit 4 stitches approximately 2" (5cm) above the bottom leaves, and repeat as for the first leaf.

Leaves Two

With color B and smallest needles, pick up 4 stitches at the left end of the obi (lower edge), at the garter ridge of the same color/fiber. Work as for Leaves One.

OBI FINISHING

Weave in all ends of the flowers.

Resists in flowers

Beginning at one edge of Flower One, in color C only, hold a marble, or other resist object, on the wrong side of the work, and secure a rubber band around the resist tightly from the right side of the work. Be sure to loop the rubber band multiple times around the object, in order to hold the resist securely. Cluster the resists as tightly as you can in the fabric of the flower, until the entire area of color C is filled with resists. Insert 1 or 2 resists into the pistol of flower (end edge in color D) and secure tightly with a rubber band.

Repeat for the other flower.

Felting

Please refer to the guidelines for *washing machine felting* on page 118. Check the felting process every 5 minutes, in order to secure a perfect fit for the obi. It is also very important to check on the obi during felting, to disentangle the ties (they will likely loop upon themselves and the ob while in the washing machine). Disentangle the ties as needed, to ensure even felting.

Allow the obi to air dry gently and slowly.

For optimum results, block obi periodically as it is drying with a cool iron to straighten (especially the top and bottom edges). Once it is fully dry, remove all resists. Iron once again for full blocking, always ironing on the wrong side of the work.

Beginning at lower edge of the flower, with coordinating yarn and tapestry needle, sew the flower in a circle, allowing the stamen to peek out at the end of the flower.

Obi Closure

If desired, 2 additional hook and eye closures can be added. Try on the obi to determine where to place the closures, based on desired fit for the waist. Use a sewing needle and thread to sew them in, making invisible stitches on the obi. Tie obi as desired.

portrait scarf

Recently, I resumed weaving—after many

years of not having access to a loom—

and discovered the concept of woven shibori.

This reentry into weaving presented the

opportunity to think about the principles of

traditional shibori that might successfully

translate into knitting.

My first few attempts at a ruffled scarf

almost *worked.*

On the cast-on end of the scarf, the ruffle

looked great; however, the opposite end of the

piece consistently came out

rather limp in contrast.

I took a gamble and threw in an extra stitch

at the end of every right-side row.

This built the previously not-so-dramatic end

of the scarf to a point, reflecting the grandeur

of the first half of the scarf.

An unexpected surprise came—the weight of

those extra stitches caused the scarf to spiral!

In the true spirit of shibori, a happy accident

led to a truly fabulous scarf.

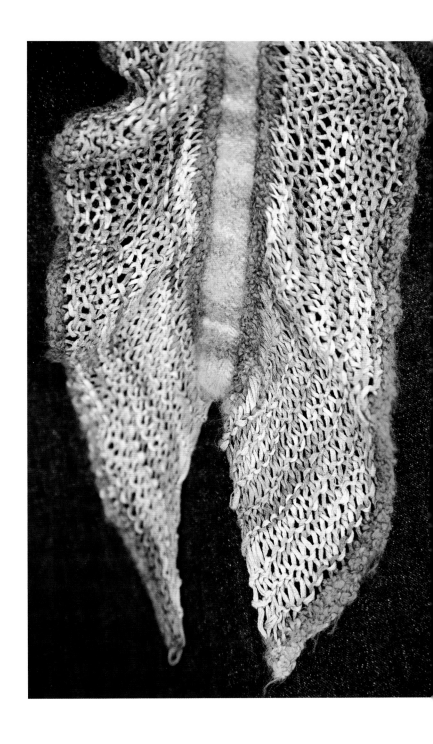

Level Intermediate

Knitted Measurements

Before felting

5½" x 84" (14cm × 213cm)

After felting

5" x 80" (12.5cm × 203cm)

Materials

Scarf on left, in photo on page 113

Felting fiber

1 skein of Alchemy Yarns Sanctuary, 70% merino, 30% silk, 1¾ oz (50g), 125 yds (114m), 53c Forest Waltz (color A), (**1**) light

Nonfelting fiber

1 skein of Alchemy Yarns Pagoda, 100% silk boucle, 1¼ oz (40g), 183 yds (167m), in 10c Costa Brava (color B), (**4**) medium

1 skein of Alchemy Yarns Silken Straw, 100% silk, 1¼ oz (40g), 236 yds (216m), 53c Forest Waltz (color C), (**2**) fine

Scarf on right in photo on page 113

Felting fiber

1 skein of Alchemy Yarns Sanctuary, 70% merino, 30% silk, 1¾ oz (50g), 125 yds (114m), 44e Cherry Tart (color A), (**3**) light

Nonfelting fiber

1 skein each of Alchemy Yarns Pagoda, 100% silk boucle, 1¼ oz (40g), 183 yds (167m), 42cc Air & Fire (color B) and 77a Dream (color C), (**4**) medium

36" (90cm) circular needle in size US 6 (4mm) or size needed to obtain gauge

A set of double-pointed needles in the same size

Crochet hook in size G-6 (4mm) or in a size that corresponds with the needles (for the optional trim)

Stitch markers

Tapestry needle

Gauge

20 stitches and 34 rows = 4" (10cm) in garter stitch using color B before felting.

Notes

The increases at the end of each right-side row in the ruffle exaggerate the pointy corner on one side. The shibori felting process naturally creates the same effect on the other side (the beginning edge).

The swirl that shows in the finished scarf will not be clearly visible until the piece is felted.

CENTER SECTION

Using color A and double-pointed needles, cast on 5 stitches and work an I-cord (see glossary, page 121) 70" (178cm) long.

RUFFLE—AUTUMNAL VERSION, ON LEFT

Side One

Using color B, pick up and knit approximately 420 stitches evenly along the I-cord (approximately 6 stitches for every 7 rows of I-cord), and knit 2 rows.

Change to color C.

Next 2 rows

Row 1 (Wrong Side) Knit.

Row 2 Knit to the last 2 stitches, kfb, k1.

Repeat these 2 rows 7 more times.

Change to color B and knit 1 row.

Bind off all stitches.

Side Two

With the right side facing, work the same as Side One, beginning the picked-up row at the opposite end of the I-cord.

RUFFLE—RED AND PURPLE VERSION, ON RIGHT

Work as for Autumnal Version Side One, except repeat the two-row pattern 8 times in total, with no color change. Bind off all stitches. Make Side Two in the same manner.

Crochet Picot Edging (optional)

Using color C and with the right side facing, work 1 round of single crochet around the entire scarf. Work 3 single crochets into each corner for the turns.

Next round *Sc into each of the next 2 stitches, ch 3, sl st into the top of the last sc; repeat from * around.

Fasten off.

FINISHING

Use a tapestry needle to weave in all the loose ends, being sure to weave at least 3" (7.5cm) of each end to ensure a tight hold during the felting process.

Felting

Please refer to the guidelines for *washing machine felting* on page 118.

Shape by hand, especially pulling out any areas that might have drawn in more tightly than desired during the felting process. Allow the scarf to air dry gently and slowly. Block it lightly to size if desired.

Finish with a cool iron on the wrong side of the work. (I recommend using a pressing towel. Stop using the towel only if you are not getting the result you want with it.) Do not drag the iron. Rather, lift and press it, focusing on the silk (nonfelting) component of the piece to flatten and soften the fibers.

fortune cookie scarf

Dynamic movement is one of the many qualities shibori

techniques impart to knitwear. Thin layers of silk knit

fabric are beautiful when put through the felting process.

The fiber itself does not felt, but it does transform—

especially in the way each stitch relaxes

while in the washing machine.

The end result is a garment of exquisite drape,

which is translucent and unique.

Two simple pieces of different sizes are knit, and then

sewn together in this happy design. Loose, flowing layers

of silk overlap in two different colors and are highlighted

with a felted mohair accent in a complementary color,

upon which rests a delightful silk crocheted ruffle in

a fourth color. The scarf may be worn in a number of

exciting ways, each of which forecasts a

bright future!

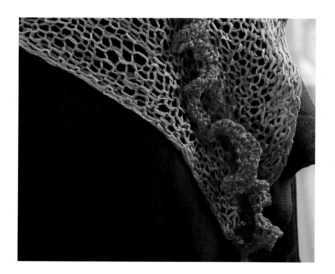

Level Intermediate

Knitted Measurements (before felting)

Smaller Side

Back length: 28" (71cm)

Width from tip to tip: 40" (102cm)

Larger Side

Back length: 38" (97cm)

Width from tip to tip: 46" (117cm)

Knitted Measurements (after felting)

Approximate width from tip to tip, with both pieces sewn together: 54" (138 cm)

Smaller Side

Back length: 18" (46cm)

Width from tip to tip: 35" (89cm)

Larger Side

Back length: 24" (61cm)

Width from tip to tip: 42" (107cm)

Materials

Nonfelting fiber

1 skein each of Alchemy Yarns Silken Straw, 100% silk, 1¼ oz (40g), 236 yds (216m), in 13a Raspberry Crush (color A) and 06f Poppy (color B); and 2 skeins in same fiber of 46f Blood Orange (color C), (**2**) fine

Felting fiber

1 skein of Alchemy Yarns Haiku, 60% mohair, 40% silk, ⅞ oz (25g), 325 yds (114m), 38a Foxglove (color D), (**2**) fine

24" circular needle in size US 10½ (6.5mm) or size needed to obtain gauge

Crochet hook size D-3 (3.25mm)

Tapestry needle

Gauge

12 stitches and 16 rows = 4" (10cm) in stockinette stitch using two strands of Silken Straw held together before felting

Notes

Two mitered pieces of slightly different sizes are knit in a nonfelting, double-stranded fiber in simple garter stitch. The pieces are worked separately, then sewn together. The front edges of the joined pieces, the miters of each piece, and the place where the two pieces are sewn together are all embellished with a

felting fiber (which will shrink when put in the washing machine). Finally, a ruffle of nonfelting fiber is worked on the final rounds of the felted embellishment.

Smaller Side

With knitting needle and color A, cast on 99 stitches.

Next row (Wrong Side) Knit.

Setup row (RS) K49, place marker, k1, place marker, k49.

Next row and all wrong-side rows Knit.

Next row (Decrease Row) Knit to 2 stitches before marker, ssk, sl m, k1, sl m, k2tog, knit to end.

Repeat the last two rows until 41 stitches remain. Bind off all stitches.

Left Wing

With knitting needle, right side facing, color A, and starting at the top left corner of the mitered piece, pick up and knit 22 stitches along the left side of the mitered piece (see diagram).

Next row (Wrong Side) Knit.

Next row (Decrease Row) K1, ssk, knit to end of row.

Work in garter stitch (knit every row), decreasing 1 stitch every 4th row as in the Decrease Row, until 3 stitches remain. K3tog. Fasten off.

Right Wing

Using the top width of the Left Wing as a guide, measure the same distance from the top right corner of the mitered piece along the right side and place a marker.

With knitting needle, right side facing, color A, and working from the marker to the top right corner, pick up and knit 22 stitches along the right side of the mitered piece (see diagram).

Next row (Wrong Side) Knit 1 row.

Next row (Decrease Row) Knit until 3 stitches remain, k2tog, k1.

Work in garter stitch, decreasing 1 stitch every 4th row as in the Decrease Row, until 3 stitches remain. K3tog. Fasten off.

Larger Side

With knitting needle and color C, cast on 125 stitches.

Next row (Wrong Side) Knit.

Setup row (Right Side) K62, place marker, k1, place marker, k62.

Next row and all wrong-side rows Knit

Next row (decrease) Knit to 2 stitches before marker, ssk, sl m, k1, sl m, k2tog, k to end.

Repeat the last two rows until 59 stitches remain. Bind off all stitches.

Left Wing

With knitting needle, right side facing, color A and starting at the top left corner of the mitered piece, pick up and knit 30 stitches along the left side of piece (see diagram).

Next row (Wrong Side) Knit.

Next row (Right Side) K1, ssk, knit to end of row.

Work in garter stitch, decreasing 1 stitch every 4th row as described, until 3 stitches remain. K3tog. Fasten off.

Sew to Left Wing
of Smaller Side

23" 21½"

38" 24"

Larger Side

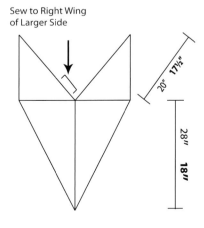

Sew to Right Wing
of Larger Side

20" 17½"

28" 18"

Smaller Side

Right Wing

Using the top width of the Left Wing as a guide, measure the same distance from the top right corner of the mitered piece along the right side and place a marker. With knitting needle, right side facing, color A, and working from the marker to the top right corner, pick up and knit 30 stitches along the right side of mitered piece (see diagram).

Next row (Wrong Side) Knit 1 row.

Next row (Right Side) Knit until 3 stitches remain, k2tog, k1.

Work in garter stitch, decreasing 1 stitch every 4th row as described, until 3 stitches remain. K3tog. Fasten off.

Sew Sides Together

Lay the two pieces on a flat surface. Place the left side wing of smaller piece next to the right side wing of larger piece. Pin pieces together from corner where wings start to 4" (10cm) toward the centers of the two mitered pieces. Sew this section with a tapestry needle and nonfelting fiber. This seam is meant to fall on the shoulder.

Note: The bottom edges of the 2 pieces should NOT align (they are meant to be different lengths). The ends of both pieces will be loose, not sewn together, which allows for overlapping of the two pieces, particularly after felting.

Center Front and Neck edging

With knitting needle, right side facing, and color D, begin at the tip of the Right Wing on the smaller mitered piece and pick up and knit approximately 110 stitches around entire front opening (the outer wings and long top edges of the two mitered pieces, now joined together).

Work 2 rows in garter stitch. Bind off all stitches.

With wrong side facing, crochet hook, and color B, work 1 row of single crochet in bound off stitches.

Next row Turn and work 2 single crochets in each single crochet of previous row.

Next row Turn and work 3 single crochets in each single crochet of previous row.

Fasten off.

Shoulder Edging

With knitting needle, right side facing, and color D, begin at the tip of the larger side's Right Wing and pick up and knit approximately 44 stitches (ending at the shoulder seam). Work 2 rows in garter stitch. Bind off all stitches.

With crochet hook, wrong side facing and color B, work 1 row of single crochet in bound-off stitches.

Next row Turn and work 2 single crochets in each single crochet of previous row.

Next row Turn and work 3 single crochets in each single crochet of previous row. Fasten off.

With knitting needle, right side facing, and color D, begin at the top of the shoulder seam and pick up and knit approximately 42 stitches (ending at tip of the smaller side's Left Wing). Work 2 rows in garter stitch. Bind off all stitches.

With crochet hook, wrong side facing, and color B, work 1 row of single crochet.

Next row Turn and work 2 single crochets in each single crochet of previous row.

Next row Turn and work 3 single crochets in each single crochet of previous row. Fasten off.

Miter Detail

With crochet hook, right side facing, and color D, work one row of single crochet along the miter (center line) of smaller piece, beginning at the point and working to the top (neck) edge.

Turn and work 1 single crochet in each single crochet of previous row.

Next row: Turn, change to color B, and work 2 single crochets in each single crochet of previous row.

Next row: Turn and work 3 single crochets in each single crochet of previous row. Fasten off.

Repeat for miter detail on larger piece.

FINISHING

Weave in all the loose ends, catching down at least 3" (7.5 cm) of each end to ensure a tight hold during the felting process (Remember: only the obi is felted).

Felting

Please refer to the guidelines for *washing machine felting* on page 118. Check the felting process every 5 minutes.

Allow the scarf to air dry gently and slowly.

Iron for blocking and softening of fiber, always ironing on the wrong side of the work.

appendix

Technical Shibori Felting Concepts

Important general characteristics of shibori felting:

1. Garter stitch shrinks more in width than height.

2. Stockinette stitch shrinks more in height than width.

3. Felting fibers generally shrink and nonfelting fibers generally grow during shibori felting. The finished result will depend on the proportion of each type of fiber worked together in a single design.

4. The golden rule: You can always felt more, but you can never undo your felting. So err on the side of underfelting and check on the felting process often!

5. Most felted pieces will expand before they shrink. Keep this in mind as you check your felting process every five minutes.

NOTE: All gauges given in the book are prefelting only.

Pre- and post-felting measurements and schematics are given for each piece, when applicable.

Washing machine felting

I recommend a top-loading machine set at the lowest water setting, hottest temperature, the gentle cycle (lowest agitation), and adding a tiny bit of quality liquid detergent. Place the item to be felted in a lingerie bag or similar washer-friendly container, if desired. Different fibers felt at different rates. After 5 minutes, if no felting progress has been made (or more likely, if your piece has actually grown significantly, which is normal for the first cycle), reset the machine and repeat the gentle cycle for 5 minutes. If there is still no change, repeat a third or fourth time. Tremendous change can happen in a very short time. Switch setting to a regular cycle (heavier agitation) only if four gentle cycles do not render a fused fabric. Continue to check every 5 minutes until the desired result is achieved. The lingerie bag is especially helpful when felting I-cord in the machine. When I-cord is long and left to beat aimlessly about in the felting process, it will knot. There will be a discernable difference in the knotted and unknotted I-cord (usually, the knot acts as a bit of a resist).

When you are satisfied with the felting result (or are not sure if it's felted enough and want to see it dry), take out the garment, rinse it in cool water, press it between a couple of towels to blot, and let it air dry. Be sure to lay it on a flat surface or as described in the pattern (around a bowl for a hat, for instance). I place my drying felts near a floor furnace vent (in winter) or outdoors (in the summer).

Also, try a practice run if you haven't felted much before or you don't know your washing machine well. Set the machine as recommended, and leave the top open. The water level will be set low, so you won't make a splashing mess. At the end of the gentle cycle with the top open, check to see if the machine stops itself before going to spin (my machine won't spin if the top is open). This is a great tool in monitoring the length of felting time your piece experiences. If your machine does proceed directly to the spin cycle, be prepared to stop it, as spinning is not a friend of shibori felting.

I recommend tracking the time your piece spends in the felting process with a portable kitchen timer. This is an indispensable tool for any kind of felting, and it frees you from hovering over the machine during the felting period.

One last word about machine felting: While it is not impossible to felt in a front-loading machine, it is messier and can be more tricky. All my friends who own front-loaders come to my house when they want to felt!

Hand felting

Though none of the projects specifically call for hand felting, there are times when it is helpful to know this is an option. Small things—I cord details, or perhaps if you want to be certain of a belt's fit, or ensuring something is the exact length desired—can be more easily controlled when hand felting. I don't recommend it for larger pieces, but for small things, it's great.

To hand felt, work in a clean sink. Adjust the water temperature to very warm, but not so hot you run the risk of burning your skin. Wet the fabric thoroughly. Then simply rub the piece between your palms, working a small section (no more than 4"–5" [10cm–12.5cm]) at a time. Continue to work small sections until the entire piece meets your felting needs. Though this practice takes more time than machine felting, it offers more control. Rinse the piece, blot with towels, and allow to dry as described for machine felting.

Patience

Remember, shibori requires patience. I know that cultivating patience is not always easy. But it is imperative for the success of shibori. I find it helpful to remember an old Chinese proverb: "One moment of patience may ward off great disaster." Insert the word "knitting" just before "disaster" for an appropriate shibori mantra! Remember: You can always felt more, but you cannot un-felt. Always err on the side of underfelting!

Debunking myths about felting

Myth # 1: Felting always shrinks.
Not with shibori. If you have added nonfelting fiber to your piece, the work may actually grow after felting. Trust that I have taken that information into account when writing these designs. If felting fiber is used exclusively, the work will surely shrink. And when a nonfelting fiber is double-stranded with a felting fiber, the two held together will also shrink—the felting fiber overpowers the nonfelting one. But if the felting and nonfelting fibers are worked side by side, which is how several of the designs in this book are written, not every part will shrink. The amount of growth or shrinkage depends on which fiber type is used in greater proportion. If you knit something that has mostly felting fiber, it will shrink. If you knit something that calls for mostly nonfelting fiber, it will grow.

Myth # 2: Heaviest agitation equals better felting.
Nope. Again, shibori is its own animal. Many of the designs in this book recommend a felting fiber that is a subtle blend of silk and wool. Such blends respond more positively to gentle agitation. It may take a little longer—two or three five-minute cycles in the machine. This gives you more control and more opportunity to achieve the quality of fabric you desire. More important, it does not stress the nonfelting fibers. Heavier agitation puts your nonfelting fiber at risk for substantial stress and possible fraying, depending on the fiber used.

Finishing after felting

Finishing is where the magic often happens with shibori. Particular characteristics of fibers will make themselves known before, during, and after the felting process. Contrary to felting lore, silks make great shibori companions to felting fibers (as they do not felt or shrink); however, many silks appreciate an ironing to soften them again after going through the rigorous process of felting. Begin with a cool iron (use the silk setting; most modern irons have this notation). Working on the wrong side with a pressing cloth (a soft, all-cotton, light-colored dishtowel), place the iron (never drag!) on the fabric. If the desired result is not achieved, remove the pressing cloth and try again on the wrong side of the work. If you are still not achieving the desired effect, work carefully on the right side of the work, being careful not to drag the iron.

Things Are Not What They May Seem

Letting a piece air dry *completely* before making decisions about the success of the piece is very important. These are the very words I wrote in my sketchbook in response to felting the Wood Grain Scarf (but before allowing it to dry fully): "UGLY!!! Make it again in a different fiber. What a waste of time." And my initial response after pulling the first Portrait Scarf out of the machine: "TOTAL BUST! I am in despair."

But I looked at the Wood Grain Scarf again after it had dried and completely changed my mind. As for the Portrait Scarf, I later went back and wrote in my book, "WRONG!! It is WAY COOL! Make it again!!!!"

The point is to let your work dry before deciding if you like it or not.

Care of Shibori knits

Though I am generally not a fan of dry cleaning, I do recommend it for shibori knits that have employed significant resist techniques (The Wood Grain Scarf or the Happy Colored Marbles Scarf, for example). If you wash this kind of shibori knitwear, the memory (or resist shaping) will be washed out of the garment. For the pieces that use little resist, and rely on the ruffling effect (Portrait Scarf, Contemplative Wrap), a gentle handwash in cool water is fine. Just be sure not to use hot water and agitation, unless you are intentionally trying to shrink the piece further.

Tips and Advice for Successful Shibori

Here are some really helpful tips to make your shibori path more enjoyable.

• A dropped stitch in a washing machine is a felting disaster. It is very difficult to recover from this mishap. Here is my advice. Before felting, if you suspect you might have dropped a stitch (and even if you don't think you have), hold your piece up to a window or a bright light. Turn it around, over, upside down, and inside out. Look for the telltale signs of a dropped stitch: a gap in the knit fabric, a loosened stitch, or an obvious run. If you find a dropped stitch, drop everything and fix it! Happily, dropped stitches are very easy to correct (and hide!) if you are felting your piece. My somewhat lazy method is as follows: If the dropped stitch is only a few rows back, rip and reknit. If the dropped stitch is several inches of fabric back in the knit, especially in Fair Isle or something complicated to unwind, try this instead: Take a darning needle and matching yarn and weave about 6" (15cm) of one end of the yarn on the wrong side of the work. Go through the dropped stitch with the needle, catching it with the yarn, then pull the yarn back to the wrong side of the work and weave in about 6" (15cm) of the other end. After the piece is felted you will never know the dropped stitch was there.

• When I knit I-cord, I find it much faster to use double-pointed needles. Time is saved by not shoving stitches across a long needle when a short needle will suffice.

• Keep a hearty supply of stitch markers in your knitting quarters. The kind that can be detached mid-row are my favorites (either the ones that snap open, or the spiral-shaped ones that do not close fully). Stitch makers are great tools if you drop a stitch and need to hold it until later. They are very useful for marking distances and helping in achieving accurate measurements.

• Choose your yarns and their fiber content carefully. Avoid working with yarns that contain the duo-blend of mohair and wool, or fibers of all wool content. I know this is what most people use for felting, but it is not appropriate for felting shibori. These fibers tend to get very fuzzy after felting. Fuzziness may be your personal aesthetic, but it is not the aesthetic for which these designs are written. The fuzzy yarns hide the subtleties shibori provides. Mohair and silk blends make a great shibori fiber, as long as the mohair component is greater than the silk component (60% mohair or more). Wool and silk is fabulous, remembering again that, to felt, the wool content has to be 60% or more. So watch out for the standard felting yarns that are made of mohair and wool, or even all wool, unless you are okay with losing detail and getting not-so-subtle fabric as your finished product. Remember, content counts.

• Some of these designs call for winding out a double-stranded ball of yarn. Check out the sidebar on page 27 for detailed instructions for an easy way to make a double-stranded ball of fiber.

• Keep a knit journal. Write down the practical stuff—how long you felted your swatch, what the fabric looks like, how much it shrinks, etc. Write down your responses to your work as you knit and as you felt—it's very entertaining! It's also a great way to see how you tend to process the world. Make it a practice to write down the logical details as you knit, such as exactly where you stopped knitting, so you know where to begin when you pick the piece up the next time. Despite good memories and even better intentions, we can easily forget where we are in a project.

• Let the piece dry before you decide if you like it or not. You knit. You felt. You hope. You pull that thing that smells like a wet dog out of your washing machine—and it can look scary. Don't despair. Let it dry. I promise this is helpful information about felting and life. Not the wet dog drying in order for you to like it bit—but wait awhile before deciding if something is your cup of tea, and give that tea a chance to steep. You might change your mind. In shibori matters, it is likely that the felted piece will change its appearance as it finishes its final transformation, which is to dry.

• Opportunity comes in clever disguises. Be patient, open-minded, and allow your shibori experience to be a wonderful metaphor for your life.

Glossary

ch   chain

k   knit

k2tog   knit 2 stitches together

k3tog   knit 3 stitches together

kfb   knit into front and back of stitch

m1   make one

p   purl

p2tog   purl 2 stitches together

rep   repeat

RS   right side

sc   single crochet

sl   slip

sl st   slip stitch

ssk   slip 2 stitches individually as if to knit them. Insert left hand needle back into these stitches and knit them together through back loop

WS   wrong side

yo   yarn over (yarn around needle).

Common knitting stitches and concepts used

garter stitch
Worked flat: Knit every row.
Worked in the round: Knit one round, purl one round.

stockinette stitch
Worked flat: Knit every right-side row; purl every wrong-side row.
Worked in the round: Knit every round.

seed stitch
Worked on an even number of stitches:
Row 1: *K1, p1, repeat from * to the end.
Row 2: *P1, k1, repeat from * to the end.
Worked on an odd number of stitches:
All rows: *K1, p1, repeat from * to last stitch, k1.

i-cord construction
Note: It is easiest to work an I-cord on double-pointed needles, but a circular needle also works.

Cast on the required number of stitches (usually 3 or 4 stitches, and rarely more than 5). *Do not turn your work. Instead, slide the stitches to the right end of the needle and knit them by pulling the working yarn around behind them. Be certain to pull the yarn tight when you make the first stitch on the next row, as you are creating a little stockinette stitch tube by knitting in one direction only. Repeat from * until the cord measures desired length.

yarn substitution guide

The following guide, organized by weight, details all Alchemy fiber used in this book, as well as comparable substitute yarns. Please be advised that only Alchemy fiber has been tested in these patterns, and no assurance can be given to the success of any substitute fiber, given the nature of shibori. Please visit www.alchemyyarns.com for information on all Alchemy yarns. All yarns used in the book have either been felted or subjected to the felting process, and all felting yarns have differing characteristics, as do nonfelting fibers. Be aware that significant changes in appearance may result if yarns are substituted, given the focus on blends of fibers used in this book.

If you choose to use a substitute fiber, please pay careful attention to gauge, and always make a swatch to ensure you have a good weight substitute. Not only should gauge match in your swatch, but you want to create a fabric that will be similar in drape, texture, and appearance of the recommended fiber. Base your yarn amount needs on total yardage, rather than skein recommendations, if you choose to substitute.

Fine (Sport, Baby)

Alchemy Haiku: Kid Silk Haze by Rowan; Kid Merino by Crystal Palace; Lace Mohair by Karabella; Kid Mohair by Louet; or Kusa by Habu Textiles, or other mohair/silk blend of comparable weight.

Alchemy Silken Straw: Bamboo Soft by Rowan; 4-Ply Cotton by Rowan; Cotton Flake by Ironstone; or other fingering weight mercerized cotton or bamboo.

Light (DK, Lighted Worsted)

Alchemy Bamboo: Baby Georgia by Crystal Palace; Dream by Tahki Yarns; Skinny Majestic by Grand River, or other cellulose (plant) fiber of comparable weight .

Alchemy Furry Kindness: Alpaca Pure or Monarch by Alchemy Yarns; Angora by Suss; Belangor by Joseph Geller; Sport Weight Alpaca by Frog Tree Yarns; or any angora/alpaca blend of comparable weight.

Alchemy Sanctuary: Cascade 220 by Cascade Yarns; Kersti Merino Crepe or Painter's Palette by Koigu; O-Wool Classic by Vermont Organic Fiber; or any 30% silk/70% merino blend fiber of a comparable weight. NOTE: Be very careful substituting this fiber, as simply matching weight will not render the finished fabric as shown.

Alchemy Silk Purse: Pima/Tencel by Cascade Yarns; Interlude by Classic Elite; La Luz by Fiesta; or any pure silk or linen yarn of comparable weight.

Medium (Worsted, Afghan, Aran)

Alchemy Pagoda: All-Season Cotton by Rowan; Cork Chenille by Habu Textiles; Dyed or Organic Cotton by Blue Sky Alpacas; Cotton Stria by Manos del Uruguay; or any boucle pure silk of comparable weight.

Alchemy Synchronicity: Lion and Lamb by Lorna's Laces; Pima/Silk by Cascade; Stormy by Classic Elite Luxury; or any silk/merino blend of comparable weight.

Bulky (Chunky)

Alchemy Wabi-Sabi: Handspun Semi-Solids by Manos del Uruguay; Lumpy Bumpy by Farmhouse Yarns; Revelation or Shephard Bulky by Lorna's Laces; Simply Heaven by Tilli Tomas; or any silk/wool blend of comparable weight.

Super Bulky (Bulky, Roving)

Alchemy Lux: Bulky Handpaints or Naturals by Blue Sky Alpaca: Cascade 109 by Cascade Yarns; or any 30% silk/70% merino blend fiber of a comparable weight. NOTE: Be very careful substituting this fiber, as simply matching weight will not render the finished fabric as shown in this book.

yarn weight symbol & category name	fine	light	medium	bulky	super bulky
other names of yarns	sport, baby	DK, light worsted four-ply, jumper	worsted, afghan, aran	chunky, craft, rug	bulky, roving
knit gauge range in stockinette stitch to 4 inches (10cm)	23–26 stitches	21–24 stitches	16–20 stitches	12–15 stitches	6–11 stitches
recommended needle size range	U.S. 3–5 (3.25–3.75mm)	U.S. 5–7 (3.25–4.5mm)	U.S. 7–9 (4.5–5.5mm)	U.S. 9–11 (5.5–8mm)	U.S. 3–5 (8mm and larger)

Alchemy Yarns of Transformation can be found at these retailers around the world.

Alaska

A Weaver's Yarn
1810 Alaska Way
Fairbanks, AK 99709
907-374-1995
www.littleshopoart.com

Arizona

Jessica's Knits
10401 E. McDowell Mountain
Ranch Road, #7
Scottsdale, AZ 85255
480-515-4454
www.jessicasknits.com

California

A Mano Yarn Center
12808 Venice Blvd.
Los Angeles, CA 90066
310-397-7170
www.amanoyarn.com

Alamitos Bay Yarn Co.
174 N. Marina Drive
Long Beach, CA 90803
562-799-8484
www.yarncompany.com

Article Pract
5010 Telegraph Avenue
Oakland, CA 94609
510-595-7875
www.articlepract.com

Bella Yarns of Sonoma
521 Broadway
Sonoma, CA 95476
707-939-2767

Compatto Yarn Salon
2112 Wilshire Blvd.
Santa Monica, CA 90403
310-453-2130
www.compattoyarnsalon.com

ImagiKnit
3897 18th Street
San Francisco, CA 94117
415-621-6642
www.imagiknit.com

Knit Café
8441 Melrose Avenue
Los Angeles, CA 90069
323-658-5648
www.knitcafe.com

Knitterly
#1 4th Street
Petaluma, CA 94952
707-762-9276
www.knitterly.net

Knitting Arts
14554 Big Basin Way
Saratoga, CA 95070
408-867-5010
www.goknit.com

Lori's Frames, Fibers, & Frills
2206 Alpine Blvd.
Alpine, CA 91901
619-659-9784

Stash
1820 Solano Ave.
Suite B-2
Berkeley, CA 94707
510-558-YARN
www.stashyarn.com

The Swift Stitch
402 Ingalls Street
Suite 12
Santa Cruz, CA 95060
831-427-9276
www.theswiftstitch.com

Wildfiber
1453 E. 14th Street
Santa Monica, CA 90404
310-458-9000
www.wildfiber.com

Colorado

Knitty Cat
7475 East Arapahoe Road #15
Centennial, CO 80112
720-493-5648
www.knittycat.com

Serendipity Yarn & Gifts
105 N. Railroad
Buena Vista, CO 81211
719-395-3110
www.serendipityyarn.com

Connecticut

Country Yarns
327 No. Colony Road
Wallingford, CT 06492
www.countryarns.com

Knitting Central
582 Post Road E.
Westport, CT 06880
203-454-4300
www.knittingcentral.com

The Knitting Niche
115 Mason Street
Greenwich, CT 06830
203-869-6205
www.knittingcentral.com

Sit 'n Knit
10 LaSalle Road
West Hartford, CT 06016
860-232-9276
www.sit-n-knit.com

Village Wools
2279 Main Street
Glastonbury, CT 06033
888-633-0898

The Yarn Barn
1866 Litchfield Turnpike
Woodbridge, CT 06525
203-389-5117
www.theyarnbarn.com

Florida

Anneke's Needleworks
7440 SW 50th Terr.
Suite #107
Miami, FL 33155
305-665-6222
www.annekesneedleworks.com

Georgia

Main Street Yarns
16 N. Main Street
Watkinsville, GA 30677
706-769-5531
www.mainstreetyarns.com

Idaho

Handmade: Your Creative
Expression
118 E. State Street
Eagle, ID 83616
208-938-8341
www.handmadeeagle.com

Isabelle's Needleworks
351 Leadville Avenue North
Ketchum, ID 83340
208-725-0408

Mountain Knits
275 E. Little Avenue
Driggs, ID 83422
208-354-4648

Illinois

Chix with Stix
7316 West Madison Street
Forest Park, IL 60130
708-366-6300

String Theory Yarn Co.
485 N. Main Street
Glen Ellyn, IL 60137
630-469-6085

Unique Yarns
7969 Forest Hills Road
Loves Park, IL 61111
815-282-5481
www.uniqueyarnsinc.com

Indiana

Knit Stop
3941 East 82nd Street
Indianapolis, IN 46240
317-595-5648

Mass Ave Knit Shop
862 Virginia Avenue
Indianapolis, IN 46203
317-638-1833
www.massaveknitshoponline
.com

Stitches & Scones
120 N. Union Street
Westfield, IN 46074
317-896-4411
www.stitchesnscones.com

Louisiana

Garden District Needleworks
2011 Magazine Street
New Orleans, LA 70130
504-558-0221

Knits by Nana
5055 Capital Heights Avenue
Suite A
Baton Rouge, LA 70806
225-216-9460
www.knitsbynana.com

Maine

Unique One
2 Bay View
Camden, ME 04843
www.uniqueone.com
207-236-8717

Yardgoods Center
60 West Concourse
Waterville, ME 04901
207-872-2118

Maryland

Crazy for Ewe
22715 Washington Street
Leonardtown, MD 20650
301-475-2744
www.crazyforewe.com

Woolworks
6117 Falls Road
Baltimore, MD 21209
410-377-2060
www.woolworksbaltimore.com

Massachusetts

Black Sheep Knitting
1500 Highland Avenue
Needham, MA 02494
781-444-0694

Colorful Stitches
48 Main Street
Lenox, MA 01240
www.colorful-stitches.com

Cranberry Quilters
161 Bay Road Rt. 1A
South Hamilton, MA 01982
978-468-3871
www.cranberryfiberarts.com

Sheep to Shore
14 Sparks Avenue
Nantucket, MA 02554
508-228-0038

Twin Hearts
137 North Street
Pittsfield, MA 01201
413-499-0021
www.twinheartshandworks.com

Northampton Wools
11 Pleasant Street
Northampton, MA 01060

Michigan

Knit Around Yarns
2663 Plymouth Road
Ann Arbor, MI 48105
734-998-3771
www.knitaround.com

The Knitting Room
251 E. Merrill Street
Birmingham, MI 48009
248-540-3623

Threadbear Fiber Arts Studio
319 S. Waverly Road
Lansing, MI 48917
517-703-9276
www.threadbearfiberarts.com

Minnesota

Needlework Unlimited
4420 Drew Avenue South
Minneapolis, MN 55410
612-925-2454
www.needleworkunlimited.com

The Yarn Garage
2980 West 145th Street
Rosemount, MN 55068
651-423-2590
www.yarngarage.com

Nevada

Nancy's Quilt Shop
3290 N. Buffalo Drive
Las Vegas, NV 89129
702-839-2779
www.nancysquiltshop.com

New Hampshire

Fiber Studio
161 Foster Hill Road
Henniker, NH 03242
603-428-7830
www.fiberstudio.com

New Jersey

A Good Yarn
200 Browerton Road
West Paterson, NJ 07424
845-913-6547
www.agoodyarn.net

Knit 1 Purl 2
345 Route 9 South
Manalapan, NJ 07726
732-577-9276

Knit Knack
1914 Springfield Avenue
Maplewood, NJ 07040
973-763-6066

The Knitting Lab
3 Claremont Road
Bernardsville, NJ 07924
908-204-9900

Modern Yarn
32a Church Street
Montclair, NJ 07042
973-509-9276
www.modernyarn.com

Wooly Lamb
7 Tree Farm Road
Unit 103
Pennington, NJ 08534
609-730-9800
www.thewoolylamb.com

New Mexico

Oodles
411 W. Water Street
Santa Fe, NM 87501
505-922-2678

New York

Annie & Company
1325 Madison Avenue
New York, NY 10128
212-360-7266
www.annieandco.com

Brooklyn General Store
128 Union Street
Brooklyn, NY 11231
718-237-7753
www.brooklyngeneral.com

Cire Knitting Salon
193 Brower Avenue
Rockville Centre, NY 11570
516-764-1240

Downtown Yarns
45 Avenue A
New York, NY 10009
212-995-5991
www.downtownyarns.com

Fiber Options
221 Rensselaer Street
Rensselaer Falls, NY 13680
315-344-7600

Finger Lakes Fibers
129 E. 4th Street
Route 414 North
Watkins Glen, NY 14891
607-535-9710
www.fingerlakesfibers.com

Katonah Yarn Co.
120 Bedford Road
Katonah, NY 10536
914-977-3145
www.katonahyarn.com

Knit New York
307 E. 14th Street
New York, NY 10003
212-387-0707
www.knitnewyork.com

Knitting & Stitching
1207 First Avenue
New York, NY 10002
212-585-4200

Knitting 321
321 E. 75th Street
New York, NY 10021
212-772-2020
www.knitting321.com

Knitty City
208 West 79th Street
New York, NY 10024
212-787-5896
www.knittycity.com

Purl
137 Sullivan Street
New York, NY 10012
212-420-8796
www.purlsoho.com

The Yarn Co.
2274 Broadway
New York, NY 10024
212-787-7878
www.theyarnco.com

North Carolina

Bella Filati Luxury Yarn
275 B NE Broad Street
Southern Pines, NC 28387
910-692-3528
www.bellafilati.com

Dee's Yarn Nook
131-1 Morris Street
Blowing Rock, NC 28605
828-295-5051
www.deesyarnnook.com

Ohio

Fiber Naturell
9224 Shelly lane
Cincinnati, OH 45242
513-793-4940
www.fibernaturell.com

Temptations
35 S. High Street
Dublin, OH 43017
614-734-0618
www.knit2temptations.com

Oklahoma

Loops
2042 Utica Square
Tulsa, OK 74114
918-742-9276
www.loopsknitting.com

Oregon

Angelika's Yarn Store
2110 North Lake Road
Lakeside, OR 97449
541-6759-3975
www.yarn-store.com

Gossamer The Knitting Place
550 SW Industrial Way
Suite 28
Bend, OR 97702
541-383-2204
www.gossamerknitting.com

Yarn Garden
1413 SE Hawthorne
Portland, OR 97214
503-239-7950
www.yarngarden.net

Pennsylvania

Forever Yarn
15 West Oakland Avenue
Doylestown, PA 18901
215-348-5648

Knit One
2721 Murray Avenue
Pittsburgh, PA 15217
412-421-6666
www.knitone.biz

Knitting to Know Ewe
2324 Second Street Pike
Penns Park, PA 18943
215-598-9276

Loop
1914 South Street
Philadelphia, PA 19146
215-893-9939
www.loopyarn.com

Twist Knitting and Spinning
6220 Lower York Road
New Hope, PA 18938
215-862-8075

Puerto Rico

Madejas
410 de Diego Ave
San Juan, PR 00920
787-273-9658

Rhode Island

Bella Yarns
508 Main Street (Rte. 114)
Warren, RI 02885
401-247-7243
www.bellayarns.com

Fresh Purls
769A Hope Street
Providence, RI 02906
401-270-8220
www.freshpurls.com

South Carolina

Knit
7 Charlotte Street
Charleston, SC 29403
843-937-8500

Tennessee

Genuine Purl
140 N. Market Street
Chattanooga, TN 37405
423-267-7336
www.genuinepurl.com

Rainbow Yarns & Fibers
1980 Exeter Road
Germantown, TN 38138
901-753-9835
www.rainbowfibres.com

Threaded Bliss Yarns
127 Franklin Road
Suite 140
Brentwood, TN 37027
615-370-8717
www.threadedbliss.com

Texas

Hill Country Weavers
1701 S. Congress
Austin, TX 78704
512-707-7396
www.hillcountryweavers.com

Yarns 2 Ewe
603 West 19th Street
Houston, TX 77008
713-880-KNIT

Utah

Black Sheep Wool Co.
430 East S. Temple
Salt Lake City, UT 84111
801-487-9378

Needlepoint Joint
241 25th Street
Ogden, UT 84401
801-394-4355
www.needlepointjoint.com

Virginia

Knit Happens
127A N. Washington Street
Alexandria, VA 22314
703-836-0039
www.knithappens.net

Washington

Hilltop Yarns
2224 Queen Anne Avenue North
Seattle, WA 98109
206-282-1332
www.hilltopyarn.com

Holy Threads
620 S. Washington
Spokane, WA 99204
509-838-0779
www.holythreads.net

Tricoter
3121 E. Madison Street
Seattle, WA 98112
Telephone:206-328-6505
Toll Free:877-554-9276
tricoter@tricoter.com

Wisconsin

The Knitting Room
74 S. Main Street
Suite 101
Fond Du Lac, WI 54935
920-906-4800

AUSTRALIA

Threads & More
141 Boundry Road
Bardon, Q4065
Brisbane
61-7-3367-0864
www.threadsandmore.com.au

CANADA

Art of Yarn
102–3010 Pandosy Street
Kelowna, BC V1Y 1W2
250-717-3247
www.artofyarn.com

Lettuce Knit
66 1/2 Nassau Street
Toronto, Ontario
M5T 1M5
416-203-9970
www.lettuceknit.com

Make One Yarn Studio
841 1st Avenue N.E.
Calgary, AB T2E-0C2
403-802-4770
www.make1yarns.com

Needles & Pins Inc.
205 Oxford Street E. #103
London, Ontario
N6A 5G6
519-642-3445
www.needlesandpins.ca

Sew Easy
15-5755 Cowrie Street
Sechelt BC V0N 3A0
604-885-2725

Urban Yarns
#1-4421 West 10th Avenue
Vancouver, BC V6R 2H8
604-228-1122

Village Yarns
4895 Douglass Street W.
Toronto, Ontario M9A 1B2
888-343-8885
www.villageyarns.com

SWEDEN

Knitlab AB
Rosenlundsgatan 38 F
11853 Stockholm
46 8 668 28 60
www.knitlab.com

UNITED KINGDOM

Get Knitted
Unit 2b Barton Hill Trading
Estate Herapath Street
Barton Hill
Bristol BS5 9RD
UK
0117 941 2600
www.getknitted.com

loop
41 Cross Street
Islington, London
N1 2BB
UK
020 7288 1160
www.loop.gb.com

gratitude and acknowledgments

I bow to the following people, offering my most humble thanks to:

Erin Slonaker, Rosy Ngo, and Chi Ling Moy at Potter Craft/Random House.

Yoshiko Wada, for her love and devotion to shibori, and for being so kind.

Photographer Lise Metzger, for capturing shibori in a truthful and poetic way. Thanks also to Alexandra Grablewski for the beautiful interior shots.

Sylvia Bors, trusted friend and sister-in-law, for photography advice and talking me out of my tree numerous times.

Linda Roghaar, my wonderful literary agent, who always lets me stand on my own two feet while steadying me quietly underneath.

Shiri Mor, technical editor extraordinaire (and very cool person), and Tanis Gray for leading me to Shiri (and other good experiences!).

The amazing group of strong, beautiful, intelligent and funny women (and one baby) who gathered graciously to model: Janel Audette, Veronica and Olivia Blaustein, Tessa Grul, Miriam Goldstein, Jill Edwards Minye, Irma Spars, and Karen Watkins. A special thanks to The Little Man, Lou Reed Wilde, who was our dashing and cooperative canine model.

Sara Webb for the glorious hairstyling, Janel Audette, for the splendid makeup, and Tessa Grul for assistance with wardrobe.

Jennifer and John Webley and family, for the use of their home in Occidental, as well as Ocean Song Farm and Wilderness Center in Occidental, CA, for the photography locations.

My knit team: Cathi Arfin, Lauren Lax, Jenny Maliki, Sandi Rosner, and Dylan Wilde. A very special shout out to Sandi, for the superlative math skills, meticulous editing, and amazing trust.

Alchemy's many wonderful retail partners around the world.

Charles Miedzinski and all faculty, staff, and fellow students of the Arts and Consciousness Department at John F. Kennedy University, Berkeley, California; Lon Anthony, my college mentor; and the irrepressible Beverly Wallace, who taught me to knit.

Modest Mouse, Joanna Newsom, Bright Eyes, Radiohead, and Austin's piano.

Clara Cabrera, my beloved friend and brilliant studio assistant. Hannah Gallagher, Lyndsey Roush, and Marilyn Webster for their years of dedication to the Alchemy work family.

The good doctors, nurses, and technicians at the Breast Care Center of the University of California at San Francisco, and the Redwood Radiology Oncology Center.

The Quilt Collective. Spring always comes. It follows winter, it precedes summer, and nothing has yet to stop it. All blessings for helping me remember and trust. Cathi Arfin, Amy Berman, Hannah and Heather Blanton, Sylvia Bors, Clara Cabrera, Stacy Cohen, Lauren Lax, Jenny Maliki, Natalie Marcrum, Wenda Marrone, Clara Parkes, Witt Pratt, Lori Sacco, Mare Smith, Ellen Webster, Marilyn Webster, and all The Wilde Ones—Adrienne, Allison, Ann Austin, Austin, Clio, Cis, Dylan, Jennifer, Susan, and Sylvia.

My grandmothers, Thelma and Estelle, for their resilience, generosity, and unfathomable courage.

My parents, Kay Webber and Jan Webber, for everything they always did and continue to do to love me; and my parents-in-law, Ann and Bill Wilde, for loving me as one of their own. Sister Shawn Webber Kipfer for her daily emails of light and love, and for always believing in me.

My sun and my moon and my stars—Clio and Dylan and Austin. If I were to write an entire book based on the topic, I could never express my love and gratitude to you three, who make me whole. Thank you for your compassion, patience, and trust.

about the author

Gina Wilde is internationally acclaimed for creating spectacular colors and luxury blends of fiber in her line of elegant hand-painted natural yarns, Alchemy Yarns of Transformation (www.alchemyyarns.com). Wilde, who holds a Master's Degree in Arts and Consciousness, is an innovative knitwear designer whose work has appeared in *Hand Knit Holidays*, *The Knitter's Book of Yarn*, *Folk Knits*, and *Interweave Knits* magazine. The daughter of a talented painter and a former beauty queen, Wilde is a renowned speaker on the topics of color, knitting, and transformation. In the course of her career, she has been a sculptor, weaver, musician, studio arts teacher, performance artist, and an arts administrator.

Wilde lives in the country an hour north of San Francisco, with her family, including her beloved partner, Austin, two amazing daughters, Dylan and Clio, and a menagerie of animals. She enjoys playing guitar, flower gardening, and traveling to faraway places, internal and external.

index

Page numbers in *italics* indicate illustrations.

A

Abbreviations, 121
Agitation level, 119
Angora, 48
Animal protein fibers, 14

B

Baby sling, *54,* 55–59
Bags
    beaded ruffle, *50,* 51–53
    Koi, *36,* 37–41
Beaded ruffle bag, *50,* 51–53
Bead embellishment, 53
Belt, op art, *64,* 65–66, *67*
Bonnet and booty set, 46–49, *47*
Bouquet wrap, *20,* 21–22, *23*
Bracelet, as variation on capelet, 85

C

Cabochon resists, 21
Care tips, 120
Changing direction, 11–12
Children's bonnet and booty set, 46–49, *47*
Color key, 96
Contemplative wrap, *92,* 93–96, *97*
Control, surrendering, 18–19
Cork resists, 33
Creativity, 44

D

Double dog dare you capelet, *84,* 85–86, *87*
Dropped stitches, 79, 120
Dry cleaning, 120
Drying, 121

F

Fassett, Kaffe, 83
Fedora, *68,* 69–71
Felted-resist method, 10–11
Felting
    of angora, 48
    fiber behavior during, 12–13
    fiber content in, 14
    finishing, 119–120
    by hand, 118–119
    shrinkage and, 119
    tips for, 120
    by washing machine, 118
Felting fiber, vs. nonfelting, 14

Felting fiber substitutions, 14, 124
Fez, *72,* 73–75
Fiber
    behavior of, 12–13
    felting vs. nonfelting, 14
    nonfelting fiber substitutions, 14
    selection of, 120
    yarn content, 13–14
    yarn weight, 13
Fiber combinations, 44
Fiber content, 13, 120
Fiber retailers, 125–127
Fiber substitutions, 14, 124
Finishing, 119–120
Form follows function, 75
Fortune cookie scarf, 114–117, *115*

G

Garter stitch, 61, 121
Gauges, 118, 124
Golf ball resists, 25

H

Hand felting, 118–119
Handpainted yarns, 13
Hand warmers, *88,* 89–91
Hand washing, 120
Happy colored marbles scarf, *24,* 25–27
Hard resist, 10
Hats
    bonnet and booty set, 46–49, *47*
    shibori fez, *72,* 73–75
    ska fedora, *68,* 69–71

I

I-cord construction, 121
Interconnectedness, 102
I wanna hold your hand warmers, *88,* 89–91

K

Kimono, 103–108, *109*
Knit journal, 120–121
Knitting stitches, 121
Koi bag, *36,* 37–41

L

Lace patterns, 91
Lap blanket, *92,* 93–96, *97*
Little bear's bonnet and booty set, 46–49, *47*

M

Marble resists, *24,* 25–27
Memory, 63
Mohair blends, 120
Mokume, 29

N

Natural resists, 12
Nonfelting fibers
    as resists, 11
    as substitutions, 14

O

Op art belt, *64,* 65–66, *67*

P

Poet's shawl, *76,* 77–79
Portrait scarf, *110,* 111–113
Purses. *See* Bags

R

Rain of fish, 41
Resists
    cabochons, 21
    corks, 33
    hard, 10
    marble, 25
    in nature, 12
    nonfelting fibers as, 11
    removal of, 22
Retailers, 123–125
Ripping out technique, 47

S

Scarf de triumphe, *60,* 61–63
Scarves
    fortune cookie, 114–117, *115*
    happy colored marbles, *24,* 25–27
    portrait, *110,* 111–113
    wine lover's, *32,* 33–35
    wood grain, *28,* 29–30, *31*
Seed stitch, 121
Shaped-resist textile, 10
Shawl, poet's, *76,* 77–79
Shibori
    characteristics of, 118
    history of, 10
    as illustrated in nature, 12
    memory in, 63
    technical felting concepts in, 118
    as transformation, 12
    types of, 10–12

Shibori fez, *72,* 73–75
Shrinkage, 119
Silk blends, 120
S'il vous plait kimono, 103–108, *109*
Ska hat, *68,* 69–71
Skirt, wild side, *98,* 99–102
Sling, for baby, *54,* 55–59
Stitches, 121
Stitch markers, 120
Stockinette stitch, 121
Substitutions, 14, 124
Subtlety, 82
Sullivan, Louis Henry, 75
Surrender, 18–19
Swatching, 14–15

T

Technical concepts, 118
Tie-dye, 10
Transformation, 12

W

Warp and weft, 11
Washing-machine felting, 118
Washing tips, 120
Weaving, 111
Whole heart baby sling, *54,* 55–59
Wild side skirt, *98,* 99–102
Wine lover's scarf, *32,* 33–35
Wood grain scarf, *28,* 29–30, *31*
Wrap and turn technique, 38, 90
Wraps
    bouquet, *20,* 21–22, *23*
    contemplative, *92,* 93–96, *97*
    for dogs, *84,* 85–86, *87*
    poet's shawl, *76,* 77–79

Y

Yarn content, 13
Yarn-held-double technique, 27
Yarn retailers, 123–125
Yarn substitution guide, 124
Yarn weight, 13, 124